Cold Crime

How police detectives
solved Alaska's
most shocking cases

by Tom Brennan

illustrations by Brian Sostrom

EPICENTER PRESS
Alaska Book Adventures™

This book is dedicated to the men and women in blue,
the police officers of Alaska

Epicenter Press is a regional press founded in Alaska whose interests include but are not limited to the arts, history, environment, and diverse cultures and lifestyles of the Pacific Northwest and high latitudes. The press seeks both the traditional and innovative in publishing nonfiction titles, and contemporary art and photography gift books.

Publisher: Kent Sturgis
Acquisition Editor: Lael Morgan
Editor: Ian Shuler
Proofreader: Sherrill Carlson
Cover and text design: Victoria Sturgis
Illustrations, maps: Brian Sostrom
Printer: Transcontinental

Library of Congress Control Number: 2005934956

ISBN 978-0-9745014-4-1

To order single copies of COLD CRIME, mail $14.95 plus $4.95 for shipping (Washington residents add $1.60 sales tax) to Epicenter Press, PO Box 82368, Kenmore, WA 98028; call toll-free 800-950-6663; or visit us online at www.EpicenterPress.com.

First edition October 2005

10 9 8 7 6 5 4 3 2

Printed in Canada

The text pages for the first printing of 5,000 copies of COLD CRIME were printed on 2,872 pounds of recycled, acid-free paper with 50% post-consumer content. According to the Green Press Initiative, of which Epicenter Press is a supporter, use of this recycled paper made it possible to conserve 17 mature trees (averaging 40 feet tall and 6-8" in diameter), 7,137 gallons of water, 1,546 pounds of net green house gases, and 2,870 kilowatt-hours of electricity. For more information about the GPI, visit www.GreenPressInitiative.org.

CONTENTS

OTHER BOOKS
BY TOM BRENNAN

Moose Dropping & Other Crimes
Against Nature

Murder at 40 Below

 PREFACE

The principal sources for this book were retired police detectives of Alaska. With help from Colonel Tom
Anderson, former director of the Alaska State Troopers,
and from the State Trooper Museum in Anchorage, I
was privileged to interview investigators who worked
on many notorious crimes.

As my research progressed, I began to understand
what motivates top police investigators, what attracts
them to their profession, and how they do their jobs. I
questioned several officers, including my son, Officer
Tobin Brennan of the Soldotna Police Department, then
on assignment as an investigator for the State Troopers'
statewide drug and alcohol enforcement team.

All agreed that police work offers the excitement and
satisfaction of putting oneself in harm's way in service to
the public. Most police jobs are intellectually challenging.
Some require great patience and tolerance for digging up
clues and doing repetitive interviews that may seem to go
nowhere. With time and persistence, the slow going often
brings results. Hidden or discarded evidence can be uncovered and understood with creative thinking. Asking the same
question again and again in recast form often trips up the
guilty. As one investigator put it, "People can tell the same
truth over and over, but lies are hard to remember."

Detectives often spend shift after shift on surveillance or sifting through records. Many crimes go unsolved, and in some cases the investigators are certain
they know who committed them but are unable to find
links that tie the suspect to the crime. In the most
frustrating cases, the detectives and prosecutors take their
evidence to court, and a judge or jury finds it unconvinc-

ing. Sometimes the investigators are wrong, and sometimes they are right and just can't prove it.

The top detectives have an ability to relate to people, to understand their quarry, to think the way the criminal thinks, and to sympathize and gain a suspect's confidence. The detectives are curious, observant, and tenacious. They notice small things that are out of place and will doggedly pursue clues, even when other officers say the evidence just isn't there. Others may decide prematurely that their favorite suspect is the guilty one, a decision that can cause the investigator to miss evidence that would lead in unexpected directions and perhaps point to another suspect entirely.

The down side is that detectives sometimes must immerse themselves in the details of horrendous murders. But even these can have satisfying moments, especially if the investigators are able to slam the jail doors behind the killers. Many top detectives are brilliant and driven, often to the detriment of their private lives. But their intensity, intelligence, and people skills pay dividends. They anticipate their opponent's moves and their interview techniques are practiced and carefully crafted to put the suspects at ease. They can back their opponents into logic corners, places from which the stumbling criminal cannot retreat. Often the suspect's resolution crumbles, resulting in confessions and cooperation that can lead from one participant to another, rolling up an entire gang. .

Some crimes are especially hard on the investigators, judges and prosecutors, and even the defense attorneys. Alaska State Trooper Sergeant Don Church, who investigated the crimes committed by undertaker Gordon Green, found it necessary to ask permission of the parents of a deceased child to borrow an urn containing their infant's ashes. Church took it to the state crime lab, which found metal scraps from adult teeth and portions of large bones, obviously not the remains of a child. "And I had to tell them," he said.

ACKNOWLEDGMENTS

This book would not have been possible without the assistance and cooperation of many people. Special thanks are due to Major Walt Gilmour, a retired Trooper and fellow author (*Butcher, Baker,* 1991, Onyx Books); retired Deputy Public Safety Commissioner Jim Vaden, retired Trooper Sergeant Don Church, Trooper Ron Costlow, retired Trooper investigators William Hughes and Major Dean Bivins, retired Trooper Sergeant Dave Kaiser, retired FBI agents Billy G. Andrews, Joe Hanlon and Stu Godwin, Anchorage Police Captain Ron Rice, and Joseph E. Young, business manager of the Alaska Peace Officers Association and a retired Anchorage Police Officer.

My thanks also go to Lew Williams Jr., retired publisher of the *Ketchikan Daily News,* and historian Louise Harrington, who supplied information for the chapter on "Ketchikan Burning"; Chris Von Imhof, who lived through the robbery at Alyeska Resort and reviewed a draft of that chapter; to friend and computer consultant Howard Marsh and the Fraternal Order of Alaska State Troopers, to friend and publisher Kent Sturgis of Epicenter Press; and to my editor Ian Shuler.

I grateful, too, for the patience and cooperation of the staffs of the Alaska Court System and the Alaska Department of Public Safety, and especially to Sharon Palmisano and Lynn Hallquist of the *Anchorage Daily News* Library; and to Sheila Toomey, whose reporting for the *Daily News* set a new and higher standard for crime and court coverage in Alaska.

chapter one

Ketchikan Burning

---

*An arsonist was loose. To keep Ketchikan
from going up in flames, off-duty
police and firemen made night patrols.
Buildings were checked hourly.
Every alarm box was dusted with dye.*

In the 1950s, Ketchikan was a quiet fishing and mining community on Southeastern Alaska's Inside Passage. Some of its residents — the fishermen and miners — were sometimes an unruly bunch, but their misbehavior consisted primarily of bar brawls and boisterous visits to Creek Street, a cluster of whorehouses built over the water on pilings. The joke around town was that that Creek Street was where both the salmon and the fishermen went to spawn. Despite the well-deserved reputation of some of its rough-hewn citizens, the town was quite civilized.

Ketchikan had fewer than six thousand people and for years had been a slow-growing town, especially after decline of the mining industry, but by 1954 a large pulp mill was under construction at Ward's Cove to process trees cut in the surrounding Tongass Forest. Lucrative jobs were coming available both at the logging end in the forest and in the manufacturing work at the mill. The excitement lifted Ketchikan's spirits; new construction sprang up everywhere, giving the place an unfamiliar feeling of things happening. Construction transformed Front Street, a sleepy thoroughfare whose greatest claim to fame was being the first paved road in Alaska.

Heavy equipment widened streets to accommodate logging trucks and engineers punched a tunnel under Knob Hill to provide quicker access to the new mill site. For the first time, high-rise apartment buildings loomed over a low-profile town of two and three-story structures. New schools were on the drawing boards and the U.S. Forest Service paid to have roads opened through the thick tree stands north of town. The new roads opened up land for home sites, cabins and church recreation sites.

Despite the promise of affluence and the building boom, the coming tax revenues hadn't begun to flow and the town couldn't afford some of the things it needed, such as a professional fire department. It relied instead on volunteers. Those who battled blazes were an important line of defense against a dangerous enemy. Ketchikan was a waterfront community of closely spaced wooden buildings. Like those on Creek Street, many were perched atop wooden pilings; the dry planks and siding in the business district were shielded from the frequent rains and were quite dry. As the town fathers knew, they could easily go up in flames. Many houses were on hills hard by the stores and offices. They were reached by wooden stairways that everyone called streets.

The twenty-seven volunteers who manned the hoses and fire trucks knew the risks their community faced. When the alarm went off, they raced to the licking flames and flooded them with water. Through the years, Chief Ralph Bartholomew and his volunteers managed to keep things under control and there were no major disasters and no loss of life. Skeptics said it was just a matter of time.

The department had plenty to keep it busy. Ketchikan was experiencing a series of small fires, all seemingly caused by carelessness. Most erupted in laundry or utility rooms when lighted candles were left near trash, though why anyone would leave a lighted candle near combustible trash was something of a mystery. The town had electric lights; candles weren't needed for much besides romantic dinners. After the first few fires many of the volunteers began to suspect the candles were placed deliberately. They became convinced somebody was setting the fires, somebody who might be delighted if the town actually did go up in smoke.

None of the blazes were serious until May 21, 1956, when an entire block went up, destroying the Coliseum Theater, the Red Men's Lodge, the Ketchikan Meat Co., and Ralph's Liquor Store. Then, on New Year's Day in 1958, the waterfront exploded in flames that raced through a dozen offices. Gone were the Alaska Steamship ticket agency, a music shop, the telegraph office, the Rainbird Café and Bar, a drugstore and a row of apartments on the second floor. The firemen rescued one panel in a series of oil paintings depicting the Shooting of Dan McGrew from the classic Alaska poem by Robert Service, but most of the panels were destroyed. The surviving painting was moved to the Sourdough Bar farther down the block.

The fire problem slowed in 1959 and people put it out of their minds. They were preoccupied with Ketchikan's growing pains. On January 12, 1960, the unknown firebug struck again and flames erupted from the Hunt Building near the tunnel entrance. The fire bell rang and volunteers raced to the scene with their trucks and hoses, dousing the blaze and saving the building. But thirteen days later a fire broke out there again and the building was destroyed, along with the rest of its neighbors on the same block. For the first time in history, Ketchikan had unobstructed views of several portions of the Tongass Narrows from Front Street. The town was undergoing a perverse kind of urban renewal.

The cumulative cost of the property losses was climbing and Chief Bartholomew was worried. He asked for help from Police Chief Hank Miller and State Fire Marshal Jerry Phillips. The three men formed themselves into an arson squad and each assigned investigators to look into the fires. The team also called in the FBI and a special agent of the National Board of Fire Underwriters.

The initial list of suspects included virtually all six thousand of Ketchikan's citizens, but the arson squad knew that the fires didn't fascinate them equally, nor were many directly involved in any capacity. The investigators began systematically reducing the list of possible suspects. At first that was an easy job, but after the initial vetting, the number of citizens left as potentials was long. The FBI ran background checks on what its report described as "a goodly portion of the city's population." It also investigated leads from New York to Hawaii.

Ketchikan was uneasy about the presence of the unknown firebug and what he or she might do. To keep the city from going up in flames, off-duty members of the fire and police departments organized night patrols. All buildings in the fire areas were checked hourly and every fire alarm box in the city was dusted with a powder dye that would stick to the hands of anyone who pulled the lever.

The detective team was puzzled by the fact that there seemed to be no motive for arson. The investigators did exhaustive checks of all the recent blazes to see if there might be one or more fraud scams in the works. But they were skeptical about the possibility; there were no likely suspects and hardly anyone stood to gain from the disasters. Insurance companies already had cancelled most policies in Ketchikan because of the fires. Nor was some kind of revenge likely since there were so many diverse and unrelated property owners.

On August 13, 1960, the detectives found their first clue. Someone set a fire in an apartment building and used a candle as a triggering device. The candle was recovered intact. The team decided to revisit the possibility of fraud and reviewed all fire records dating back to 1943. They developed a new list of possible suspects and State Trooper Ed Dankworth, the state's only polygraph expert, flew down from Anchorage to give lie detector tests to more than one hundred residents and property owners. Every test came up negative.

Squad members settled for a time on one man who seemed a likely suspect. They put all their resources into a two-week investigation of the man, who never was named publicly. The suspect eventually was cleared and the frustrated investigators decided to begin again, trying another tack.

The FBI report said lack of a motive or a clear pattern for the fires convinced the arson squad that it was dealing with a true pyromaniac, somebody who set fires because he found it thrilling and probably got a sexual charge out of the act. Under such circumstances, the first place investigators look is to those who are closest to the fires and involved in the battle against them — the volunteers who man the trucks and hoses. The detectives were by no means certain they would find their arsonist there, but it was a logical place to look. Though little was known about pyromania, it was not unheard of for those with the depraved disorder to gravitate to fire departments.

The arson squad asked Fire Chief Bartholomew for permission to investigate his volunteers and requested that state troopers send Dankworth back to Ketchikan to use his lie detector expertise on members of the fire department. Dankworth returned and on the evening of August 27, 1960, the volunteers were asked to report for polygraph examination the next morning. That same evening a department lieutenant suddenly became ill and went to his doctor for medical treatment. He was admitted to the hospital next morning. When he was released he left the state for a short rest.

Lieutenant William Henry Mitchell and ten other firemen were unavailable when the lie detector tests were given. All sixteen who did take the exam passed it easily. The other ten were absent for various reasons, but the arson squad was especially interested in Lieutenant Mitchell because of his sudden illness. They learned from his doctor that his medical emergency was caused by an overdose of drugs. The team began looking into all of the department's records of past fires and drills, especially those involving Mitchell.

Bill Mitchell was one of the department's most enthusiastic members. Despite his appearance of innocence, the investigators kept running across his trail in ways that surprised them. He did his volunteer duties well and was always the first to arrive at each fire no matter what the fire's distance was from his store; he seemed extraordinarily excited by the blazes and the damage they caused. Isobel Daigler, manager of the Coliseum Theater, recalled how the "nice young fireman" always came by to talk to her at the theater after the fires and seemed so exhilarated by them — at least he did until the theater burned down.

Ketchikan people considered Mitchell to be a fine young man. He was popular, handsome, married to an attractive Pan American World Airways stewardess, and was active in the community. He was president of the Junior Chamber of Commerce. His mother and stepfather were the well-liked owners of the Ben Franklin store, which Mitchell managed for them. He loved his volunteer work and the spiffy uniform he wore on formal occasions. When the fire bell rang, he would throw on his equipment, lock the store, and run. He was frequently injured or overcome by smoke, and sometimes wound up being treated at the local hospital, each time getting headlines and much attention.

The investigators grew increasingly certain that Mitchell was their firebug, though their joint detective effort turned up no solid proof. The slim leads they ran across included the fact that the candle found at the August 13 apartment house fire was a kind Bill Mitchell sold in the Ben Franklin. The investigators worried whether they might be wrong about their suspicions. If they were wrong, and they accused him, Mitchell's parents and his wife would be humiliated needlessly. Some of his fellow volunteers became aware of the team's suspicions but couldn't believe Mitchell could be the firebug. He was one of them and a friend who ate dinner at their homes. But such fires in the tinder-dry downtown worried everyone. Bud and Pat Charles, owners of the *Ketchikan Daily News*, lived in an apartment over the newspaper plant and — just in case the arsonist struck again — sent their three children to live with relatives in another part of town, where they would be safer.

On January 25, 1961, another serious fire erupted in downtown Ketchikan. The blaze ruined the mortuary on Main Street, burned through the second story of the 108 Bar, and ate its way into a portion of the Bon Marchè before being watered into submission. The firemen halted the flames just short of the Mitchell store. The arson squad quickly ruled out natural and accidental causes. They told Mitchell that Dankworth was back in town and asked him once more to take a polygraph examination. Within two hours Mitchell was running to catch a plane south; he said his father was seriously ill in Salt Lake City. Though the arson squad was most interested in testing Mitchell, they decided that in Mitchell's absence they would use the lie detector on the other ten firemen who had missed Dankworth's previous session. All passed.

Dankworth made a pretense of leaving, but actually went into hiding under a false name at the Ingersoll Hotel. He stayed in his room and had meals delivered to him. Dankworth quietly asked the *Ketchikan Daily News* to carry a story saying that he had gone on to Juneau. When Mitchell reappeared, Chief Bartholomew announced that the polygraph man was still in town, had successfully tested the other ten volunteers, and was ready to test Mitchell. The department's only remaining holdout said he had to check in first with his mom. He ran out of the fire station with several police officers and firemen following him. They caught him trying to swallow a vial of drugs and restrained him, but not before he had already downed part of the bottle. Mitchell demanded to be taken to the hospital, which always had been a safe haven where he went after his fire heroics, and said he wanted to talk to a psychiatrist. He voluntarily committed himself to a hospital in Juneau for treatment of mental problems.

The fire chief later told a reporter that when Dankworth wanted to administer his test Mitchell was "a foot high on phenobarbital and we couldn't do anything. But we knew he was the one." Dankworth couldn't wait for Mitchell to get over his drug poisoning; he had to leave Ketchikan on other trooper business. In his absence, the arson squad interviewed all of the volunteers and asked them to write down their recollections of various fires, where they were, what part they played in fighting each blaze, and whom they saw there. The detectives compared their notes against what Mitchell had told them and found several discrepancies.

In the Juneau hospital, meanwhile, Mitchell refused to talk to anyone except an old friend, a captain in the Ketchikan Fire Department. The captain flew to Juneau, went to the hospital and accused Mitchell of setting the fires. He presented his lieutenant with some of the evidence. The candle found at the fire was in a glass holder identical to those sold at Mitchell's parents' Ben Franklin store — and the lighted candles had been surrounded by crumpled paper that ignited when the wax burned down far enough, giving the firebug time to distance himself from the scene.

Mitchell admitted that he was the firebug.

In March, a state grand jury secretly indicted him on two counts of second-degree arson. The proceedings were kept secret to make sure he didn't disappear again. He was arrested and appeared before a Superior Court judge on May 1, pleading not guilty. His stepfather put up $7,500 bond to secure his release pending trial. With the court's permission, Mitchell went to California to stay with his wife's mother until the court hearing, scheduled for July.

In late June, a special agent from the Anchorage office of the FBI showed up in Ketchikan looking for a fugitive sought for passing a series of forged checks. He passed out circulars bearing the man's photograph and description and mentioned that the forger sometimes impersonated women. Nobody had seen anyone like that so the agent went on to other towns in Southeast Alaska.

Everyone assumed with a feeling of relief that, with Mitchell gone, the town's arson blitz was over. The big Fourth of July Celebration began on July 3. Dock Street was blocked off and filled with booths for games and sale of baked goods, candy, and anything else that might attract the eye of a reveler. Children darted through the crowds in the safety of the roped-off area. Tavern doors were propped open. All was joyous until mid-afternoon when flames erupted in the Tongass Trading building, which housed a hardware and grocery store. When firemen pushed through the crowds to the second floor, they found the building's standing fire hose had been cut. While they worked, another blaze flared in a drugstore and apartment building two blocks away, and little more than an hour later a third one erupted in a hotel across the street from the first fire, which they were still fighting. All available equipment went into the struggle. With the entire downtown threatening to go up in flames, the town fathers recruited every able-bodied person to carry hoses and help spray water. The local Coast Guardsmen joined the fight and Boy Scouts helped police in directing traffic and keeping order. The battle went on into the night. The last flames were doused at 2:20 the next morning.

Late afternoon on July 3, several hours before the fires broke out in downtown Ketchikan, the police chief had called the FBI man in Anchorage to advise him that the local Pan American ticket office had just phoned. A man dressed as a woman had picked up a ticket on its southbound flight to Seattle, possibly the check forger he was after. The ticket had been purchased earlier in Seattle and wired to Ketchikan. The man in drag was by then on his way back to the city airport on Annette Island. The Pan American employees remembered being questioned by the FBI agent and thought the man might be his missing fugitive. The chief said he talked to a taxi driver that had dealt with the suspect and the cabbie said the "woman" was a dead ringer for the person in the fugitive photo.

The FBI agent called his department's Seattle office and requested that the individual be met at Seattle-

Tacoma Airport and arrested when he left the airliner. With Pan American's help, the agents there were able to talk with the aircraft's crew in flight. They got a good description of the passenger and his seat number, and confirmed that the person definitely was a man dressed as a woman and traveling under the name Julia Dunton. When the plane arrived at its assigned gate, the flight attendants asked the passengers to remain in their places. Then FBI agents boarded the flight, went directly to Julia Dunton's seat, and took the surprised passenger into the terminal for questioning. They found it was not the fugitive in the photo but Ketchikan fireman Bill Mitchell. The agents took him to the U.S. Customs office to be photographed and then notified their colleague in Anchorage that the woman was Mitchell. The FBI agent tried to call the Ketchikan police chief, but by then the entire town had been thrown into the fight against the still-raging fires and it was all but impossible to get through. The FBI man told the telephone operator that the call was urgent and she tracked the chief down at one fire and got him to a phone.

Chief Miller was a graduate of the FBI Academy and knew what would help most in making a case against Mitchell — a photograph of the renegade fireman in Ketchikan, preferably at the time the fires were burning, and dressed like a woman. By then the holiday festivities were winding down and many people were leaving, including a large number who came from out of town. The chief put all his men to work interviewing the partygoers, looking especially for those with cameras. The FBI in Seattle took photos of Mitchell in his drag outfit for possible comparison and sent them to Ketchikan.

The intensive investigation by the FBI and Ketchikan police turned up some interesting items and proved that Mitchell's disguise had been quite good. For one, the suspect flew from Ketchikan to Annette Island on the morning of the fires traveling under the name Helen Monson. From Annette he flew the final Ellis Air seaplane hop from Annette to Ketchikan with Lloyd Tillson, the plane's pilot. Tillson was also a volunteer fireman and a good friend of Mitchell's, but the pilot didn't recognize his buddy. Tillson did remember the FBI circular and called his office to report that the bad-check artist might be in town; Pan American alerted Chief Bartholomew. Before the fires broke out, Police Officer Ray Hackstock was directing traffic and holiday celebrants at the intersection of Front and Dock streets when he saw a large woman cross the street. She was fairly attractive and seemed well dressed in harlequin sunglasses, high heels and a two-piece dress with a coat over her shoulders and carrying a large handbag. Hackstock thought she was a plus-size knockout. Fireman Wally Kubley passed the woman on a sidewalk thought she looked familiar and said hello, but she just nodded and kept on walking. Kubley shrugged and went on his way. When Mitchell returned to Annette Island for his return flight that afternoon, as unseen candles burned down toward their waiting tinder, a randy logger approached Julia Dunton in the Annette Island lounge. The logger asked for a date in Seattle and bought the visiting beauty a cup of coffee.

The firebug's total time in Ketchikan was little more than two hours, which is why he traveled under two different names. The sudden outbreak of major and simultaneous fires initially left the fire crews puzzled and worried — the volunteers didn't know what the police chief knew and assumed that Mitchell, their only known firebug, was still in California.

The FBI in Seattle could not hold Mitchell because he was free on bond and they had no new charges to place against him, so the fireman resumed his trip. Traveling under false names was unusual but not illegal. Travelers then were not required to show identification unless they paid for their tickets with a check.

Meanwhile, the Ketchikan investigators dug up what evidence was available. Though they could find no photographs of Mitchell in town during the fires, they found enough physical evidence and eyewitness testimony to indict him on additional arson charges. The next day, Mitchell's family talked him into surrendering. He called the FBI office in San Francisco and went to the Placer County Sheriff's Office, where he was arrested. He was returned to Ketchikan, held under bond of $150,000 — the highest ever set in Alaska — and confessed to starting a dozen fires. Many people suspected that, because the suspicious blazes had gone on for so many years, the actual total might have been much higher.

Mitchell pled guilty to five arson charges and was sentenced to ten years in prison. He was sent to McNeil Island Penitentiary in Washington State, served several years, and was paroled early. He behaved well in prison and won his release with the help of a Fairbanks businesswoman serving on the Alaska Parole Board. While he was at McNeil, Mitchell's wife divorced him and transferred to the Pan American base in San Francisco. After his release, the Fairbanks woman helped him find a job. He lived in Manley Hot Springs for many years, apparently kept out of trouble and — as far as anyone knows — started no more fires. Mitchell later decided he wanted to be near family members in California, so he moved there, spending the rest of his life far from Ketchikan.

chapter two

Mystery of Mendeltna Lodge

Elmer Haab got along with most of his neighbors on the Glenn Highway. He didn't drink or smoke. He was generous to friends. But there was something very wrong.

Elmer Haab was a stocky man and extremely strong. He could lift an automobile engine with his hands. His wife, Bonnie, was a laboratory technician in California before they met. Elmer was a career criminal who had served time in California, Oregon, and Washington. He had been married several times before but his strength and congenial personality attracted Bonnie. She was hazel-eyed, petite woman of five-foot-four, a delicate contrast to her hulking husband.

In 1965, Elmer and Bonnie moved to Alaska to start a new life. Bonnie may have been unaware that Elmer was violating conditions of his parole by leaving the state of California without approval. The couple borrowed five thousand dollars from Bonnie's mother in Portland,

Oregon to buy Mendeltna Lodge, a roadside bar and restaurant on a sparsely populated stretch of the Glenn
Highway south of Glennallen.

Bonnie was then forty-two; Elmer was eleven years
older. Two friends, Amiel and Emma Tooley, later joined
them and helped run the lodge. Amiel Tooley had an
extensive arrest record, too, and had met Elmer Haab
when both were serving time at Walla Walla State Prison
in Washington.

Elmer Haab got on well with most of his neighbors, and the business seemed to be going well. Most
people liked him. He didn't drink or smoke, appeared
to be an upstanding citizen, and was known to be
generous to his friends. But there were signs of
trouble. Sometimes Bonnie showed up in public with
bruises and cuts on her face, convincing some of the
neighbors that Elmer was beating her. One customer
walked into the lodge for a drink and caught Haab
slapping a tiny old man whom Bonnie had befriended
and given a part-time bartending job. Haab roughed
him up because he was convinced the man, known
as "Little Jack," was drinking more liquor than he
was selling.

Elmer Haab asked his neighbor, Joe Cretzler, for permission to store a supply of Army rations in the attic of
Cretzler's Moose-a-Boo Garage. Joe thought the request
was curious because Haab seemed to have plenty of storage space of his own. The source of the military rations
was unknown, and Haab didn't say, but Joe Cretzler often saw soldiers hunting and fishing on Mendeltna Lodge
property. Still, Joe wanted to be a good neighbor, so he
agreed to store the rations.

A few months later, Haab approached Joe Cretzler's
wife about storing cases of auto and machine parts in
the woods behind the garage. Mrs. Cretzler suspected
that the cases contained stolen goods, probably taken

from the military. She said later, "I told him his woods were just as big as our woods."

On May 30, 1966, Bonnie Haab showed up at the Moose-a-Boo with the entire left side of her face bruised and bleeding. She said she was getting out and asked the Cretzlers to hold onto seven hundred dollars in checks for her. Bonnie left and never returned. Several days afterward, Joe Cretzler drove up to the Mendeltna Lodge and found Haab standing in the parking lot beside his truck. When Haab saw Cretzler coming, he jumped into his pickup and tore out of the yard, spewing gravel behind him. The bed of the pickup was covered by a tarp.

At first Elmer Haab told the Cretzlers that Bonnie was in Montana for a vacation. Later he showed them a letter from his wife saying she never wanted to see him again. But the Cretzlers were skeptical. Among other things, Bonnie's beloved poodle was still at the lodge. They couldn't imagine she would leave her dog behind. After holding Bonnie's checks for several months, the Cretzlers contacted the Alaska State Troopers. The troopers, with no official complaint filed and having no indication that a crime had been committed, refused to get involved.

Gradually things returned to normal along the Glenn Highway. Elmer gave away Bonnie's poodle and her personal belongings. He quietly managed to get the Mendeltna property transferred from Bonnie's name to his own, despite the fact that Bonnie's mother had by then invested ten thousand dollars in the lodge. The mother had a promissory note signed by her daughter but no mortgage on the property. Though she didn't know it then, the loan was essentially uncollectible.

Not long after Bonnie's disappearance, Elmer had brought an unidentified woman to a notary's office and introduced her as his wife. The two asked the notary to draw up a power of attorney giving control of the property to Elmer's friend, Amiel Tooley. The woman signed Bonnie's name, the notary signed her own name and stamped the document, making it official. Tooley then sold the lodge property to Elmer Haab for ten dollars. Elmer also drained Bonnie's bank account and deposited all her money in his account.

In October, Bonnie's mother wrote the Alaska State Troopers expressing concern that she hadn't heard from her daughter since May. Trooper Detective Don Church from the Trooper Criminal Investigation Bureau interviewed Elmer Haab and talked to neighbors whose statements, especially those of the Cretzlers, raised his suspicions. A records check showed that Haab had a record dating back to 1935. He had been arrested for a variety of crimes, including safecracking, but none involved violence.

After being contacted by Church, Elmer Haab reported Bonnie missing with her car, though police already had found the car stripped in the parking lot of a bar. Haab's neighbors were convinced that Elmer had done something to Bonnie, but the detective could find no hard evidence. There were no indications that she had left Alaska and there was no sign of a body.

Church's dogged investigation went on in Alaska for three years. Prolonged sleuthing was difficult. The state trooper budget for expensive long-distance calls was tight, ruling out extended interviews with sources in the Lower 48. But Church was convinced Bonnie was dead and that Haab had been involved in some kind of illicit traffic in stolen goods. Bonnie had many friends in Alaska and California. To save money, Church focused on those within the less expensive calling area of Alaska.

He also did an intensive records check in all fifty states, with frustratingly little progress or encouragement.

One day the detective ran across a police report that Haab had reported a car stolen from the parking lot of an Anchorage bar at 2 A.M. Because Haab didn't drink, his being at a liquor club in the wee hours was curious enough to warrant further investigation. Church checked the records at local junkyards and found that the car reported stolen had been totaled and stripped down to its frame. The detective recorded the frame identification number and talked to the junkyard owner, who remembered the car and how it had arrived. The man said Haab did quite a bit of business with area junkyards. In fact, he was suspicious of Haab because some blank vehicle title forms had been stolen from his office the last time Haab visited.

Church checked with an auto insurance company, where an agent suggested that reporting cars stolen and then junking them could involve several crimes, including insurance fraud. Church kept following the chain of contacts of people who knew either Elmer or Bonnie. He uncovered convincing evidence that Haab had been running a multi-state ring — stealing automobiles and cases of auto and machine parts in other West Coast states, selling them in Alaska, meanwhile sending stolen Alaska merchandise southward. Church caught up with and interrogated one of the ring's wheelmen and learned in detail how it operated. The driver admitted that the Haab gang was stealing tools and robbing liquor stores in Alaska. They also stole cars and moved them in both directions on the Alaska Highway. Then the ring would buy wrecked cars similar to the stolen cars and obtain titles that made ownership of the stolen vehicles seem legitimate.

Elmer Haab had filed for divorce from his wife in 1967. The following year, he sold the lodge for its true value — somewhere between sixty-five and eighty thousand dollars. Church and two other detectives went to call on Haab in Anchorage, but somebody tipped him off, and they missed their suspect by fifteen minutes. Church put his hand on the hood of Haab's car. It was still warm. But Haab had disappeared.

Then, a piece of misdelivered mail arrived bearing a Los Angeles address.

Haab was traced to Los Angeles. Because the Haab operation by then was known to be operating across state lines, Church requested help from the FBI. Agents were sent to call on Haab in L.A. but he disappeared shortly before the agents arrived.

However, Haab couldn't stay out of trouble. Soon he was arrested for a burglary in Arizona and sent away for a five-year prison term. Sitting in an Arizona lockup, anticipating murder charges in Alaska and possible life in prison, Haab decided it was time to make the best deal he could. He wrote to Trooper Church and said he wanted to return to Alaska to clear things up.

Given a temporary release by Arizona corrections officials, Haab returned to Anchorage with Church and fellow Trooper Detective Dean Bivins. When they took their prisoner to the Phoenix airport, Haab refused to get on the plane, saying he didn't want to fly. Church looked at Haab's muscular frame.

"OK, we can take a bus to Alaska," he said, "but you'll have to be in manacles the whole way." Haab shuffled glumly onto the jetliner.

In one of several interviews, Haab finally admitted that Bonnie was dead. He said her death was an accident. She had been drunk, he said, and when he tried to put her to bed, he pushed her through a door and she fell, hitting her head on a water pump. He said he put her in bed but she was dead when he came back to check on her. Because of his criminal record, Haab said he feared being blamed for her death and decided to dispose of the body. He and a friend took the corpse to a gravel pit, piled wood and brush around it, and started a fire that they kept feeding for two nights until nothing was left but ashes. Those he shoveled into an empty oil drum. Then he raked the ground and swept it with a broom, and emptied the drum into Mendeltna Creek.

Elmer Haab's lawyer negotiated a plea bargain under which Haab would plead guilty to manslaughter in return for showing detectives where he had cremated his wife. Haab took Church and another detective to the gravel pit and the place along the creek where he had dumped the ashes. The detectives shoveled dirt from the cremation site onto a screen and sifted a few bone fragments, some ashes, and other human residue into a drum. The officers were well along in the process when they heard a "thunk." A spent .44 slug had fallen to the bottom of their metal barrel. The find was curious, suggesting that Bonnie might have been shot. She had owned a .44 magnum that disappeared when she did. But both hunters and target shooters used the gravel pit and the history of the slug could not be traced. The detectives continued sifting and assembling what little evidence remained after three years.

The evidence allowed the troopers only to confirm that Bonnie was dead and cremated. As agreed, Haab pleaded guilty to manslaughter and was sentenced to ten years in an Alaska prison, to be served after he completed his term in Arizona. He also was tried and convicted of insurance fraud for which he was sentenced another three years. Charges of grand larceny in connection with the auto-theft ring were dropped.

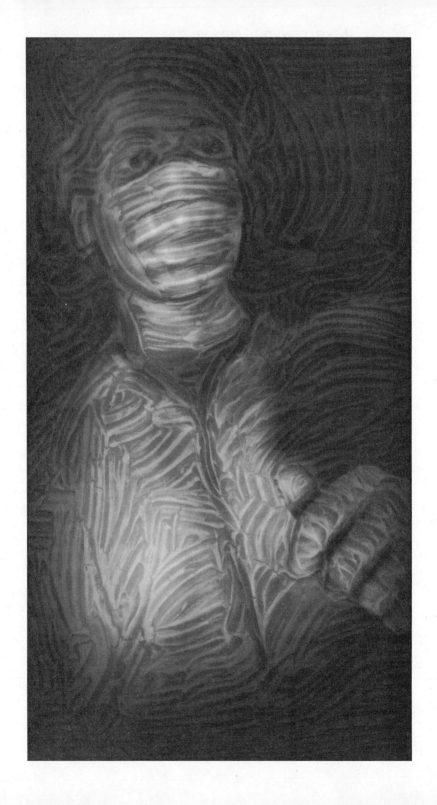

chapter three

The Deadly Dentist

---

*The vibrant young wife and mother
of three walked into the dentist's
office at 8 a.m. She came out dead.
And she wasn't the only patient to
die in the dentist's chair.*

December 12, 1967. Christmas was coming, business at the Anchorage bakery was busy, but Tom Peterson's boss gave Peterson the day off to care for his three young children while his wife, Jennifer, visited a dentist. Dr. Robert W. Smith was Alaska's only oral surgeon. The Petersons had moved from Oregon a year earlier.

Jennifer Peterson dreaded the visit because she needed extensive work. Dr. Smith's assistant had warned that Jennifer's teeth were so neglected she would need many fillings. Several teeth would have to be extracted. Some were marginal and might be difficult to save. She would be in the chair for about four hours. The assistant told the patient she would receive anesthesia and would be asleep while the otherwise painful work was done.

Jennifer was nervous as she and Tom drove early that morning toward the Medical Arts Building on Northern Lights Boulevard, one of several buildings owned by Dr. Smith. Tom Peterson would be at home with the kids, waiting for her call. He reassured her, kissed her goodbye, and watched as she walked away down the hall.

Peterson went back to their apartment and bathed their year-old son, Mark, and three-year-old twin daughters, Kerry and Shelly. Then, he washed dishes, did housework, and waited for the doctor's office to call. When he hadn't heard from Jennifer by noon he grew worried. He checked the phone and realized it was out of order. He felt a twinge of panic. "I could picture her at the dentist's trying to get a call through to me," he recalled later.

Peterson bundled the kids into the car and headed back to Dr. Smith's office. "When I didn't see my wife out front," he said, "I drove around the building and parked in the rear where I could leave the children in the car for a few minutes while I ran in and picked her up." He asked the receptionist if Jennifer was ready to go home, and the woman told him to have a seat. Tom waited a few minutes but worried about leaving the children alone in the car too long, so he went outside and brought them back to the reception area with him.

Ten minutes later, the doctor called him into his office and told him that his wife had suffered a cardiac arrest. Peterson was stunned.

"What is that?" he asked.

Dr. Smith said her heart had stopped.

"You mean she is dead?" Peterson asked.

"Yes," the dentist answered.

The young father and husband couldn't comprehend what had happened. His twenty-year-old wife was a strong and healthy young woman. She had gone through the door of the office that morning in good condition. It was unthinkable that she would never come home.

Then, the dentist said something that struck Tom as bizarre. "It's a bad time of the year for it to happen," he said.

Tom Peterson shook his head and looked at the Dr. Smith in disbelief. Any time of the year would be a bad time for your wife to die in a dentist's chair.

Dr. Smith asked if Jennifer had any history of heart trouble. Peterson said she had not, except for temporary high blood pressure when the twins were born. The dentist asked where he wanted his wife's body sent, and then went back to work on his other patients.

Jennifer's body was taken to the city mortuary, where Dr. Michael Beirne performed an autopsy. Beirne reported that the young mother's heart had failed from natural causes during the dental surgery. The young mother's death might have been written off as just one of those tragedies that befall even young people — unexpected death for unknown reasons. But a day later, a maintenance man from the Northern Lights Medical Center walked into the downtown office of the district attorney. He told Chief Assistant D.A. Bob Yandell that Jennifer Peterson was not the first person to die in Dr. Smith's dental chair.

Alaska State Troopers assigned Investigator Don Hughes to look into the case and the attorney general ordered a second autopsy, this one by forensic pathologist Dr. Charles P. Larson from Tacoma General Hospital in Washington State. The pathologist found that Jennifer Peterson's heart was normal, and that she was killed by an overdose of anesthesia. He said her death could have been prevented with proper monitoring of the patient and appropriate emergency treatment.

Hughes was a sixteen-year veteran lawman, having served in both the territorial and state police before formation of the Alaska State Troopers. He knew how to conduct an investigation. Hughes and a team of detectives dug into a variety of state and local records. They interviewed Dr. Smith's past and present employees, professional associates, and educators who supervised his dental education at Ohio State Dental College, from which he graduated in 1950, and at the Air University School of Medicine, an Air Force institution he attended in 1952.

The trooper team learned that Jennifer Peterson was the fifth patient to die during or after treatment in Smith's dental chair. The first was a three-year-old child whose heart stopped beating while under anesthesia in May of 1960, less than a year after Smith opened his Anchorage practice. The second was a six-year-old mentally retarded patient who died without regaining consciousness five weeks after oral surgery in 1961. A thirty-year-old woman also died in 1961. The fourth was Elizabeth F. Phillips of Glennallen, whose heart stopped beating while Smith performed what was to have been routine dental surgery in May 1963. Other patients reported becoming seriously ill after treatment by Smith.

On December 30, Investigator Dean Bivins and a team of uniformed troopers appeared at the clinic to serve a search warrant. Smith's receptionist said she was busy and tried to close the window to her office. Bivins grabbed the window, held it open, and climbed in headfirst. The receptionist screamed, prompting the dentist behind her to shriek as well. Bivins ignored them and opened the office door to let his fellow troopers in, then seized the anesthesia machine and other equipment.

Tom Peterson took his wife's body home to Oregon for burial while the state attorney general's office and the troopers gathered evidence for presentation to a grand jury. In mid-December, the Alaska Board of Dental Examiners and acting District Attorney Robert K. Yandell announced jointly that the dental board would assist prosecutors in investigating the deaths. On January 26, Smith was indicted by a grand jury on two counts of negligent homicide in the deaths of Jennifer Peterson and Elizabeth Phillips. He was arraigned in Superior Court that afternoon and released on a one thousand dollar bond.

As the investigation proceeded, it became clear that Smith's method of operation was reckless and extremely dangerous for his patients. Investigators learned that the common method of sedating patients in other states was to involve two professionals, an anesthetist and the dental surgeon. The practice allowed the anesthesia expert to administer the gas and monitor the patient's vital signs while the dentist worked on the patient's mouth. But they learned that Smith preferred to do both jobs himself, saving the salary of an anesthetist and keeping his overhead costs low and profit margin high. He told a co-worker that his ambition was to make a million dollars and leave Anchorage as soon as he could.

Trial on the two homicide charges began on June 4, 1968, with former Attorney General Edgar P. Boyko as special prosecutor and a three-man team led by Anchorage lawyer Stanley J. McCutcheon representing Smith. Both Boyko and McCutcheon were colorful and flamboyant men with dramatic courtroom flair. Their face-off before Judge Eben H. Lewis was guaranteed to be a classic legal battle with high news media interest.

McCutcheon tried unsuccessfully to have the trial postponed, claiming that the heavy publicity made it all but impossible for Smith to get a fair trial. He then asked for a mistrial based on news articles that contained information about the case that was not submitted as evidence and would therefore be officially unavailable to the jury.

As prospective jurors were called and questioned, McCutcheon asked for a halt and told Judge Lewis in his characteristically wounded tone, "In my thirty years in the courtroom, I have never seen a (jury) panel so steeped in gossip and radio and newspaper propaganda."

The prejudice, he added, "is reflected in their faces . . . and in their eyes."

Boyko countered that McCutcheon's argument was "an indictment against the entire jury system." Judge Lewis acknowledged that McCutcheon's impassioned motion and claim of a prejudicial atmosphere might have some merit, but he denied the request for delay or mistrial and ordered jury selection to continue and the trial to begin.

Boyko and the prosecution witnesses drew a graphic picture of what happened in Smith's office on the day Jennifer Peterson died. After Tom Peterson kissed his wife and watched her walk off down the hallway outside Smith's office at 8 A.M., Jennifer entered, was welcomed by the receptionist, and took a seat in the reception area. Dental assistant Mrs. Clytie Scott appeared and led her to one of the office's two treatment rooms, where she took Jennifer's blood pressure, asked her a series of questions about her health, and took new X-rays of her teeth. About 9:30, Dr. Smith came into the room and injected her with Seconal®, a barbiturate that slows down activity of the brain and nervous system, and Brevital®, which helps to produce relaxation, deep sleep or loss of consciousness before and during surgery.

When he was sure Jennifer was asleep, Smith ran a tube through her nose and into her throat. He then turned a valve and opened a flow of oxygen and a vapor-based anesthetic into her lungs. The dentist then went to work on her teeth, starting what he called a complete mouth restoration.

Around 10:30, a second patient was led to the adjacent operating room and Smith left Jennifer to anaesthetize the new arrival so he could pull a few teeth.

He asked Mrs. Scott and the receptionist to check on Jennifer.

For the next hour, the dentist moved back and forth between the two rooms. By 11:30, Smith noticed that Jennifer's lips were turning blue so he began squeezing an air bag to force more oxygen into her lungs. The increased oxygen returned her color and he resumed work on her teeth. But anesthesia experts testified that bagging the patient — as the procedure is called — also forced more anesthetic into her system. Smith was unknowingly making the problem worse by pushing his patient deeper under the gas even though the extra oxygen made the visible symptoms go away.

Fifteen minutes later, Jennifer's lips turned blue again. The dentist bagged her again until her normal color returned, and once again he resumed work in her mouth. After another fifteen minutes she suffered a third attack of cyanosis, but this time things took a dangerous turn for the worse — her heart stopped. The dentist tried to inject adrenaline into her body, but he had not left an intravenous needle in her arm, and his attempts failed. With her heart stopped, her veins were collapsing and becoming difficult to find. He also ran out of adrenaline and had to send Mrs. Scott to buy more at a drugstore in the building.

The dentist then began bagging Jennifer yet again with one hand while messaging her heart with the other. Expert witnesses testified that massaging her heart in the chair instead of placing her on a flat, hard surface was a hopeless and ineffective effort. Bruises showed he also was missing her heart.

Fifteen minutes later, Jennifer appeared lifeless, Smith sent for Dr. Eldon I. Maxwell, a physician with offices in the building. Both Dr. Maxwell and his physician partner were at lunch. No emergency was indicated, so Maxwell's secretary took no action. Shortly after 1:00, Mrs. Scott called Maxwell's office and said a patient was indeed having an emergency, so the secretary summoned Maxwell.

The physician raced to Smith's office and ordered a nurse to bring an electrocardiogram machine. When he arrived, Dr. Maxwell found the dentist with no stethoscope around his neck but still giving his patient a heart massage. Maxwell took Jennifer's pulse and found none, then hooked up the EKG machine. She had no sign of a heartbeat and her skin was cold to the touch. He injected adrenalin into her heart, but got no response. Maxwell complained that the dental chair made effective heart massage difficult.

Eventually he turned to Smith and asked, "Which is better for your practice, to put her in an ambulance or pronounce her dead here?"

Smith answered, "She died here."

Dr. Maxwell pronounced Jennifer dead at 1:47 P.M. and closed her eyelids. Shortly afterward, Smith met with Jennifer's distraught husband Tom, and then went back to work on his other patients.

On June 18, in the fifth week of the trial, with more prosecution witnesses waiting to take the stand, Judge Lewis announced a recess. Both sides met in Lewis' chambers and returned to the courtroom two hours later. They announced that an agreement had been reached. The negligent homicide charges would be dropped and Smith would be allowed to plead *nolo contendere* — literally, "no contest" — to two counts of assault and battery.

Two weeks later, Smith returned to the courtroom where Judge Lewis sentenced him to a six-month jail term, all of it suspended, and five years of probation. He also ordered Smith to surrender his license to practice dentistry in Alaska.

The sudden and surprising end to the high-profile case brought howls of outrage from the public and news media. Cries of "deal" were heard on the streets, on broadcast news, and in newspaper opinion columns. The uproar prompted Judge Lewis to issue a statement saying that throwing an errant medical practitioner into prison would have served no legitimate purpose, that Smith did not deliberately kill patients and it was more important to protect the public by getting him out of the practice of dentistry.

Lewis also noted that if the trial continued, its outcome might be reversed if McCutcheon successfully claimed that publicity had tainted the trial and influenced the jury. Some of the news stories had reported deaths of Smith's other patients for which no charges were brought and included information that could not have been presented to jurors.

Because of the public furor, Lewis said, "The lions had been loosened in the arena and the outcry for blood would not be abated." He added that allowing the deal was in the public interest.

Under state law, Dr. Smith's license could be suspended for only five years, so it was returned to him in 1973 but was permanently revoked in 1979.

chapter four

The Cab Driver Killer

*The hungry suspected murderer called
a Spenard restaurant from his hideout and
ordered a sack of hamburgers to be picked
up by a friend. The waitress recognized
his voice and called troopers.*

Joseph Weldon "Chuck" Roberts had an extensive police record for relatively minor crimes such as burglary, carrying concealed weapons, drunken driving, and — many times — being drunk in public. A stocky forty-eight-year-old, Chuck Roberts was well known to police in Anchorage in 1966. When he was seventeen, Roberts was charged with kidnapping after a sheriff tried to arrest him. He grabbed the sheriff's gun, commandeered the sheriff's vehicle, and made his escape. In 1946, he received an unconditional pardon, though the reasons for that act of executive clemency have been lost to history.

Despite his record, Roberts was able to obtain a license to drive a taxi. Though he kept late hours, he was married and the father of four children. Besides driving cab, Roberts ran a business on the side. When passengers were unable to pay for their ride, Roberts often took their watches or other possessions instead of cash. He accepted small television sets, guns, and cameras, but mostly watches, which could be concealed and were easier to sell in bars. He sometimes lent cash for the goods, effectively running a rolling pawnshop. Because Weldon owned his own taxi and was a contractor to Yellow Cab, the dispatcher ignored the off-register transactions. They didn't affect the company's bottom line.

Roberts peddled the merchandise in Anchorage bars, dropping in when the taxi business grew slow. He made good money selling timepieces to his fellow drinkers, so when demand outran supply, Chuck lined up a wholesaler in Los Angeles to keep him stocked when passengers with goods to pawn grew scarce.

On an April evening in 1966, Roberts dropped in at the Alley Cat Bar on Fourth Avenue for a nip before work. Afterward, he walked up an alley toward the parking lot and his cab, which he left running behind the shuttered Esquire tavern. Near the empty bar he encountered Charles Bowling, a fellow driver who was sitting in his own cab. The two men struck up a conversation and Bowling asked Roberts if he had a .357 magnum like the magnum he had borrowed and bullets for it.

Being the accommodating merchant, Roberts climbed into Bowling's car and asked to be driven to his home on Eleventh Avenue, seven blocks away. There, he grabbed a partial box of .357 ammunition from the trunk of an old car. He gave the bullets to Bowling, who loaded his borrowed pistol and stashed it away in his own car.

Roberts decided he could make more money that evening by selling watches than he could driving for Yellow Cab. He had received a new shipment of timepieces from L.A. and was anxious to convert them to cash. So, he took the night off and hired Bowling to drive him to the bars, have a few drinks, and look for sales prospects.

First they went to the Fireside Lounge in Spenard on the south side of town. Roberts had left a watch with a bartender there several days before and wanted either cash payment or the watch back. Bowling decided to wait in his cab behind the lounge, though Roberts stayed inside drinking and hawking watches for more than two hours. Eventually Roberts brought his waiting driver a vodka Collins and a beer, then returned to the Fireside for another two hours during which he occasionally brought drinks outside to Bowling.

Later they headed downtown to the Malemute Saloon, taking with them a young man who was interested in one of Chuck's flashier timepieces. Roberts wanted fifteen dollars for the watch. The man apparently thought Chuck had said *fifty* dollars and countered that he could only afford twenty. The salesman feigned reluctance but said he would settle for twenty and closed the deal. Roberts and Bowling laughed uproariously after the young man left with the overpriced watch.

Roberts and his driver went from bar to bar, selling watches and drinking at every stop. Bowling remained in the car throughout the tour, nursing the drinks Roberts brought him. After a final stop at the Roaring Twenties, Roberts returned to the taxi, climbed into the passenger's seat, and began counting his cash. He offered Bowling fifteen dollars for driving him around but Bowling grew angry and demanded more.

"No," the driver said, "I want half of the money." Bowling thought Roberts either had stolen the watches or somehow gotten them for nothing, and that all the cash in Roberts's fist represented profit.

Roberts was outraged. He made one hundred percent markup on the watches and half the cash was what he paid for them. Giving Bowling half the money would leave him with no profit at all.

"That wasn't the agreement," Roberts snarled. "The agreement was for cab fare. If you want it, you'll have to take it."

Bowling pulled the .357 from its hiding place and said: "Well, you can either give me half or I'll take it all." He cocked the pistol's hammer.

The sound of the hammer frightened Roberts. He grabbed for the gun and the two wrestled for it. The pistol went off, creating a deafening noise inside the small taxi. Roberts grabbed the gun and fired it four times. One of the shots hit Bowling in the side of the head. Chuck got out of the car, ran around to the driver's side, and tried to push Bowling over to the passenger's seat.

"Get over and I'll take you to the hospital or go get you some help," he said to the corpse.

Bowling was too heavy for Roberts to push, so he ran back to the passenger's side and tried without success to pull the body across. Then, he tried to squeeze in behind the wheel next to Bowling, but that didn't work either. Roberts didn't want to call police because of his prior record. He had the dead man's blood on his hands, on his clothes, and on the cash, so he ran away. He flagged the first taxi he saw and asked to be taken to a spot near his home, but told the driver to show his fare's destination as the Nevada Tavern. The driver wrote the Nevada into his trip log and dropped him off.

Roberts walked home with his ears still ringing from the gunfire inside Bowling's taxi. He changed clothes and left for the Nevada, throwing his bloody clothes into one garbage can along the way and the .357 into another. His own money was soaked in blood so he borrowed twenty dollars from a friend at the bar and used that money to pay for another taxi. He rode around town for a time, and then switched to yet another cab. The driver asked Chuck if he had heard that a taxi driver had been shot in the back. Roberts felt bad about the news and wanted to tell what really happened, that he and Bowling had struggled for the gun, so he went into the Montana Club and surrendered to a police officer who had stopped there on his rounds.

Roberts was arrested and eventually indicted. Police alleged that he shot Bowling while attempting to rob him. But Roberts's lawyer claimed the shots were fired in self-defense. Roberts said Bowling actually was robbing him and that he grabbed Bowling's gun and shot him repeatedly while fending off an attack. The case went to trial in August and the jury, hearing no witnesses to contradict Roberts's story, found him not guilty. The jurors either believed his claim of self-defense or decided to give him the benefit of their doubt. He was set free and returned to his driving job.

Less than five months later another driver turned up dead. Cecil L. Colvin, thirty-nine, was a former Yellow Cab driver who quit and went into competition with his former employers. His new organization was named Veterans Cab Company, a small but increasingly popular group of drivers. His wife Marcia, owner of Veterans Cab, was expecting their first child.

A Navy veteran of World War II and a former Anchorage police officer, Colvin was a dapper man who was fond of bow ties. Despite his sophisticated appearance, he was willing to do virtually whatever it took to succeed in his chosen line of work, whether that meant simply offering transportation, delivering liquor, or providing a prostitute.

On January 4, 1967, Colvin stopped at the drive-through window of a liquor store and told the clerk, a friend, that a woman had called asking him to pick up a bottle of whiskey and one of Collins mix. He was to take them to a room at the Lake Motel. Colvin drove up to the motel about 10:30 P.M. Minutes later, the manager heard three shots outside Room 9. The manager found the driver lying face down in the snow beside his cab, its engine and meter still running. He had been shot in the wrist, chest, and head. He was dead. An autopsy would show that one bullet traveled through the bridge of his nose and right eye, another cut through both wrists, and the third went entirely through his body.

The first state troopers on the scene found the driver's wallet stuffed with money. Robbery was not a motive. Among those called out was young investigator Dean Bivins, who arrived as the body was being carried away to the city morgue. A senior officer ordered Bivins to find any bullets or shell casings that might be lying on or under the snow. On a cold January night, the assignment was not a choice one. Bivins borrowed a portable Herman Nelson heater, a small furnace typically used by Lake Hood pilots to warm airplane engines in the depths of winter. He laid a canvas over the parking lot outside Room 9, weighted the corners with firewood, and pumped hot air under the tarp to melt away any snow or ice that might be covering useful evidence.

The strategy paid off. Six hours later, Bivins found a spent bullet sitting atop a small piece of ice. The detective team speculated that Colvin was shot after an argument with a passenger, but soon cast a wider net to consider other possibilities. Because of the earlier cabbie shooting, Chuck Roberts's name came to mind. But when the detectives went looking for him, Roberts was not to be found. He had dropped out of sight.

The next morning, an Anchorage woman heard her telephone make an unusual noise. The sound was not the normal ring of a telephone, just a "ding." Nema Marine was annoyed. She and her husband had ordered a one-party line but the telephone company apparently messed up the order. The couple had been hearing odd noises for several weeks. The problem was supposedly fixed, but one night their eldest son heard the ding, picked up the phone, and heard someone talking. Mrs. Marine swore angrily. The telephone company had proven once more that it couldn't keep its accounts straight. When the little ding sounded, Mrs. Marine picked up the receiver and asked, "Who is calling this number?" There was no response but she heard no dial tone and was convinced that another person was on the line; she hung up in disgust.

About 10:45 on the morning of January 5, Mrs. Marine heard the odd dinging sound again. She picked up the phone and could hear two men talking. But this time she did not hang up. She was determined to find out what was going on with her telephone.

"I've done it now," a man's voice said. "I've been shot in the knee and I need some place to rest for a while. Can you help me?"

While Mrs. Marine listened, awestruck, the second man asked, "How bad?"

"Pretty bad. I've had medical attention from a doctor who is a personal friend of mine, and treated me at his home. The doctor felt like he owed that to me."

"I don't know," responded the second man. "Call me back in a few minutes, Mr. Wilson."

"Don't tell anyone, not even my wife," the caller said, "I can't drive the car. I think I'll go to Fairbanks and sell some watches."

The second man suspected someone was listening and asked the wounded man to call back. By this time,

Mrs. Marine couldn't put the phone down. She kept the receiver to her ear and held the disconnect button down while the call was redialed. When the connection was made, she released the button and listened silently.

"I'll be in front of ... grocery store," the caller said, part of his message garbled. "Either a grocery store or there's an alley in the back. Come and look it over and see which place would be better."

The second man told his friend not to make any more calls from the phone he was using and to get to a pay phone instead. The ploy didn't work and Mrs. Marine overheard subsequent conversations as well. In one call, the wounded man referred to a .32 Special he owned, expressing concern that investigators would find it and trace it back to him.

The second man said state troopers had contacted him, but the two made arrangements to meet anyway. Mrs. Marine called police and told them what she had overheard.

The case against Chuck Roberts grew stronger when troopers learned that Room 9 was rented to "Nels" Nelson, described as a near-sighted, middle-aged man. Nelson eventually turned up drunk on an Anchorage street and told detectives that Roberts asked him to book the room, saying he wanted it for a woman.

Nelson said Roberts waited outside in the cab while he signed the motel register and brought him the room key. Roberts gave him ten dollars for his troubles and dropped him off downtown. Police were worried that Nelson would disappear, so they charged him with being drunk in public. A judge sentenced him to six months in state jail, where he was certain to be available if needed for further interviews or to testify against Roberts.

Six days after the Colvin shooting, District Attorney Tom Curran interrupted a scheduled grand jury hearing to present evidence against Roberts, who was indicted for first-degree murder. An investigator told a newspaper reporter that one of the possible motives for the latest shooting was revenge because Roberts believed Colvin had persuaded another cabbie to testify for the prosecution in the previous murder trial.

State troopers still couldn't find Roberts. They sent photos and his description to border guards, airport employees, and local police across the state. They warned that he was probably armed and should be considered extremely dangerous. A detective noted that, if the revenge theory was correct, the lives of others involved in the earlier trial could be in danger as long as Roberts remained at large. He said the missing cabbie was likely still in the Anchorage area.

Based on the conversation overheard by Nema Marine, the investigators speculated that local friends were helping Roberts. They warned that harboring a wanted felon was itself a felony and that anyone who did would be prosecuted.

Less than two weeks after the shooting, while the statewide manhunt continued, Chuck Roberts called a favorite Spenard restaurant from his Anchorage hideout and ordered a sack of hamburgers to be picked up by a friend. He gave a phony name, but the waitress taking the order had waited on Roberts and recognized his voice. The call weighed on her conscience and several days later she called troopers.

About 6 A.M. on January 19, troopers received an anonymous tip that Roberts was hiding in a supposedly unoccupied Spenard apartment. Three state officers in plainclothes showed up, finding the apartment locked. When nobody answered, Sergeant Ed Dankworth and Trooper Donald Hughes went to track down the building owner while the third, Trooper Gene Rudolph, stayed behind and watched the apartment door from his parked station wagon.

Two hours, Rudolph saw the apartment door open five inches. A head looked out at doorknob height. Moments later, the door swung wide open and a man emerged. Rudolph drew his gun and walked around a four-foot snow bank blocking his view. There on the ground, trying to crawl away, was Chuck Roberts. The missing cabbie had a .44 stuffed under his belt, but made no attempt to pull it out.

When Rudolph identified himself and told Roberts he was under arrest, the suspect said, "I'm gonna run. I'm gonna run. Are you going to give me a chance?"

Rudolph asked what kind of chance he meant. Roberts answered, "Well, I'll get running. It would be better than a shootout."

Just then, the trooper's two partners returned and Roberts went back to jail.

At Chuck Roberts's trial, his lawyer argued again that the cabbie had killed in self-defense, though the jury was not told that this would be his second self-defense shooting. Roberts testified that his passenger that January night was a Kenai oil driller in Anchorage on a bender who hired the driver to watch over him and keep him out of trouble while he got drunk.

According to Roberts, he and Colvin got into an argument when Colvin brought a prostitute to the Lake Motel. "You're getting ahead of the deal," Roberts complained. He told Colvin that the driller had a few more nightspots to hit and that he wasn't interested in Colvin's prostitute. Colvin demanded payment anyway — one hundred dollars for the woman, and fifteen dollars for his own delivery services.

"You can use her," Colvin told Roberts. But Roberts already had arranged for another prostitute. Roberts said he offered to pay for the prostitute's cab fare home. Colvin was angry by then and left with her, vowing to return and get payment.

"I was pretty mad," Roberts testified, "and I knew he was awful mad." Roberts told Colvin "when you come back, you better bring somebody along."

When Colvin left, Roberts went to his parked car, took out a .357 magnum and returned to the room. Colvin returned twenty minutes later and pushed into the hotel room with "a little bitty gun" in his hand, Roberts said later.

Roberts grabbed for Colvin's gun and the two scuffled their way outside into the parking lot, each with a pistol in his hand. Roberts disarmed Colvin and told him, "Get out of here before somebody gets hurt."

At that point, Roberts said, Colvin was crouched a few feet away and charged him. He said Colvin landed on top of him and tried to wrestle away the .357. Roberts kicked Colvin backward and fired the .357 into his head and chest, and in the process shot himself in the knee. As the shots flew, Colvin "hit the snow," Roberts said.

After the shooting, Roberts took both guns, drove home, and wrapped his wounded knee with towels. He threw his pistol into the snow near his home and hid Colvin's smaller gun under the hood of an old car behind his house. Roberts testified that he and his attorney later retrieved Colvin's gun and turned it in as evidence.

A physician from the upscale Turnagain neighborhood west of Spenard testified that Roberts showed up on his doorstep about 3 A.M. that morning with a bullet in his knee. Roberts pleaded that he was hurt and in trouble, begging for emergency treatment. The doctor said the cabbie told him he had been in a fight and accidentally shot himself.

Charles Lewis, Yellow Cab dispatcher and brother of company president Robert Lewis, testified that Roberts called him the night of the Colvin shooting and asked to see him, saying he was in trouble. Charles Lewis picked Roberts up at his home and drove him to Mountain View, where Roberts deposited a paper sack in an alley trashcan. Lewis said Roberts told him it contained bloody towels he had used to wrap his wounded knee.

Roberts told him his assailant had "charged through the door like a wounded tiger and jumped me." Lewis couldn't recall if Roberts told him that his attacker was Colvin, but he assumed that's whom he meant. Roberts told him, "I didn't intend to kill him," and that the attack was "the closest he ever came to getting killed."

Lewis drove Roberts to the home of the doctor who bandaged the knee and then dropped Roberts off at the apartment of another Yellow Cab driver.

Roberts told Lewis he didn't want to go home and face arrest in front of his wife and children. The next afternoon, Lewis picked Roberts up at the Pink Poodle, drove him to a drug store to buy bandages and medicine, and then dropped him off at another cocktail lounge. Lewis said he met with Roberts that afternoon and referred him to still another driver's apartment. Lewis said that was the last time he talked to Roberts.

Defense lawyers asked the judge to rule that Nema Marine's listening in on Roberts's phone call was an unauthorized wiretap, and that her testimony should be excluded from trial. The judge accepted it as valid evidence.

Asked in court if she had listened to the full ten-minute phone call, she said, "After I heard what I heard the first time, yes, I couldn't do anything else but listen."

During the trial, troopers submitted ballistics reports on the spent bullet that investigator Dean Bivins found in the snow outside the Lake Motel. The tests showed it was fired from Chuck Roberts's pistol and went through Cecil Colvin's body.

This time the jury did not believe Roberts's story. He was found guilty of second-degree murder and sentenced to life in prison with the possibility of parole. Roberts did not go directly to prison, however. His appeals went on for months and several times he asked to be released for a work-release program. One of his requests in January 1968 was to serve as night manager at a coffee shop near Anchorage police headquarters. The appeal noted that employees of the department frequented the coffee shop and that Roberts would therefore be under informal observation by officers stopping by for their coffee and doughnuts.

That request was denied but Roberts later was released to work days in a coffee shop operated by his wife. He was ordered to report back to jail each night after the end of his shift. The work release was rescinded a few months later when Roberts's wife complained that her husband was having daily temper fits at the restaurant and that he threatened to kill her.

Roberts's lawyers complained in another appeal that Roberts was denied a request to have two troopers accompany him on tour of Anchorage bars to gather evidence to support his appeal. The judge shook his head as he refused to order a barhopping tour.

Roberts's appeal was denied several months later and he was ordered to begin serving the long-delayed life sentence.

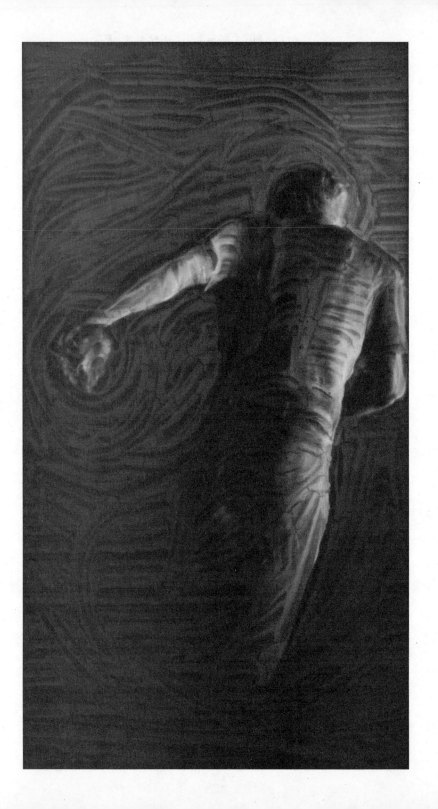

chapter five

Murders at Jackass Creek

The chief of the Alaska State Troopers liked to ask probing questions and offer unsolicited suggestions to his investigators. Had they considered the killer might be an escaped prisoner?

Lawrence Zimmerman and his employer's eleven-year-old son, Paul Hair, set out on August 14, 1971 for an easy day trip from Eagle River to Gunsight Mountain Lodge, about ninety miles up the Glenn Highway. They were expected to return by late afternoon.

Zimmerman, forty-four, worked for Jerry Hair at the electrical shop on nearby Elmendorf Air Force Base. Hair had planned to make the trip himself but couldn't make it so he sent his son instead. He thought the boy would enjoy a chance to get away from home for a day and to see some impressive scenery along the way. Zimmerman could use help from a boy with a strong back. The travelers were hauling groceries and auto parts for the lodge and planned to tow a camper trailer back to Eagle River that afternoon with Zimmerman's 1970 Toyota Land Cruiser.

When Paul was more than three hours late in returning, his stepmother grew worried and made a few phone calls. One was to Zimmerman's friends at Gunsight Mountain Lodge. She was stunned to learn that Larry and Paul had not shown up and, feeling panic, called state troopers who notified the Rescue Coordination Center at Fort Richardson. Police and volunteers cruised the highway and drove down every side road. Military helicopters and Civil Air Patrol fixed-wing planes flew over the woods and the broad floodplain of the Matanuska River. Paul's frantic dad and stepmother drove the highway, checking every lodge and service station.

The massive effort turned up nothing.

Complicating the search were torrential rains that flooded Matanuska Valley streams and rivers, washing out some roads and dumping loose gravel into waterways. Friends of the families drove through the downpour repeatedly, looking for damaged culverts or a missing guardrail where Zimmerman's big Toyota might have been swept off the Glenn Highway.

Larry Zimmerman was a rock hound and the highly respected vice president of the Chugach Gem and Mineral Society. After a few days of hunting by the military and civilian agencies, as the rains began to slacken, Zimmerman's fellow rock hound members organized their own effort. They brought friends with all-terrain vehicles, cars, horses, and an airboat that roared up and down the Matanuska River. Other volunteers combed both sides of the highway on foot. Still nothing.

State troopers were mystified. They had many questions but few answers. "If we find the vehicle," one investigator said five days after the disappearance, "we'll have the answers. We have lots of rumors, but nothing substantial."

The rumors included reports that the Zimmerman vehicle had been seen beyond Gunsight Mountain Lodge. Descriptions of the pair were sent to U.S. and Canadian border officials and to the Royal Canadian Mounted Police. The RCMP notified the Alaska State Troopers that several people along the Alaska Highway thought they might have seen Zimmerman's vehicle headed south through the Yukon Territory.

That raised new suspicions in Alaska. At the Criminal Investigation Bureau, Captain Tom Anderson ordered a background check on Zimmerman. Corporal Dean Bivins contacted everyone who knew or had contact with the man and dug through court files for any past criminal record. Nothing turned up. Although Zimmerman had a wife and daughter at home, troopers reluctantly concluded that he had taken the boy. They obtained a warrant charging Larry Zimmerman with child stealing. The report of cross-border sightings brought the FBI and RCMP into the case, but their work and combined investigation failed to turn up any useful information, nothing that would suggest where the missing pair might be.

On Saturday, August 29, a hunter hiking on Jackass Creek below the Glenn Highway found the body of a boy four hundred yards off the highway. He raced back up the slope, drove to Sheep Mountain Lodge, and called state troopers. A team was dispatched to recover the body and conduct a sweep of the area. Examination of the body confirmed that it was Paul Hair. His head was badly gashed and he appeared to have drowned.

The area was thoroughly combed that afternoon and evening, and again on Sunday morning. The troopers pushed their way through thick brush, alders, and thorns on a long and steep slope below the roadway, finding nothing. Lack of a second body suggested that Zimmerman might have smashed the boy in the head, left him dying face down in the water, and driven away. This seemed inconsistent with Zimmerman's reputation, but police work had long before taught them to consider all possibilities, even the unlikely ones.

Then, a three-man team returned to try one more time. Sergeant Walt Gilmour, newly assigned as lead investigator on the case, drove to the creek with Corporal Howard Luther and Detective Joe Hoffbeck. The detectives were not ready to accept the possibility that Zimmerman was a murderer who had escaped. For hours, the three officers worked their way across and down the slope. Wet and cold, they were close to exhaustion when they scrambled down a ravine and reached a cliff over which Jackass Creek dropped to the Matanuska River below. At the last logjam before the waterfall, Luther poked into the gravel and spotted a piece of blue jean. He tugged at it and found that the cloth covered a hand. Lawrence Zimmerman's body was covered by gravel washed down in the flood.

The body was driven back to Anchorage where Dr. Mike Beirne, a forensic pathologist, conducted an autopsy. Beirne told detectives that both the boy and the adult had suffered extreme head injuries and already were dying when they drowned in the creek. The troopers wondered at first if both might have been killed in a wreck in which Zimmerman's car left the road and their bodies were carried four hundred yards down the raging creek. There was no sign of the vehicle, but it might have been washed over the cliff into the Matanuska River where it could have been swept

downstream and buried under roiling mud and gravel.
The Toyota was large and heavy, but the rains had been
unprecedented, the flooding powerful, and anything
was possible.

As the investigation dragged on, the case drew the
attention of Colonel Ed Dankworth, chief of the Alaska
State Troopers. Dankworth was not shy about asking
probing questions and making unsolicited suggestions.
Dankworth dropped in on the trooper detectives and
wondered if they had considered whether the dead man
and boy might have picked up a hitchhiker, perhaps an
escaped prisoner who murdered them. The detectives
admitted they had not. When Dankworth left they called
all of the penal facilities in the area. The Palmer Adult
Camp reported that one of their prisoners escaped on
August 14, the day Lawrence Zimmerman and Paul Hair
disappeared.

Willis B. Mayo, Jr., twenty-one, was serving a six-
month sentence for auto theft, grand larceny, and drug
possession. He walked away from the minimum-security prison farm after being named head cook, a promotion that seemed to trouble him.

The detectives were especially interested in a piece
of fresh-cut black hair found stuck to a bloodstained
rock brought in by Zimmerman's brother. Harold
Zimmerman had gone to Jackass Creek the day after
the bodies were found, conducted his own search, and
found a bloody rock in a clump of bushes. The troopers
had missed it. The dark hair didn't match either of the
victims. The boy was blond and the short strand seemed
too dark for the graying Zimmerman. The penal farm
reported that Mayo had black hair and received a haircut shortly before he walked away.

In Fairbanks, a citizen called city police to report that a vehicle matching the description of Zimmerman's Toyota had been parked near his home for several days. Discovery of the vehicle brought Gilmour to Fairbanks to head up the investigation from there.

When Fairbanks Patrolman Jimmie Clements realized that the double murderer had come through his city, he checked his notes, remembering that he had assisted a driver whose Toyota Land Cruiser was out of gas on the day of the killings. He had no reason then to suspect the driver of a crime, so he drove him to a service station to fill a jug with gasoline and returned him to his vehicle. Gilmour mixed a photo of Mayo in with a file of others and showed them to Clements. The officer easily picked Mayo's face out of the photo lineup.

Gilmour concluded that Mayo had abandoned the car and flown out of Fairbanks the same day, though neither airline nor airport officials remembered seeing anyone matching his description. Gilmour swore out a warrant charging the escapee with two counts of first-degree murder and with one of felony joyriding.

Checks with the penal and court systems showed that though Mayo had been sent to a minimum-security facility, he had a long criminal record. He had a history of mental illness and several suicide attempts, including one in which he was found hanging and might have suffered brain damage. The investigators entered the warrant information and Mayo's description into their newly acquired computer system, which was linked to the National Crime Information Center, a huge database used by police agencies nationwide.

Meanwhile, a detective called Willis Mayo's mother in Portland, Oregon. Mrs. Mayo said that her son had visited briefly and left. Soon after the call, a patrol officer in Bellingham, Washington, stopped a car for a minor traffic infraction. Inside were three men and two women, including Mayo, who was revealed to be a fugitive in the NCIC database. Mayo was arrested on the spot and taken to a holding cell to await transport back to Alaska. The other four were released.

At that point, the case took a bizarre turn when the Fairbanks district attorney complained about what he saw as interference by Walt Gilmour, the Anchorage-based trooper who had taken over an investigation in the Fairbanks Police jurisdiction. The district attorney sent an angry letter to his supervisor. The letter was bucked up the chain to the governor, and then sent to Ed Dankworth and back down to Gilmour. Knowing that the heat was on, Gilmour's fellow officers kidded him that he had better get a confession from Mayo quickly or his career was likely to be shortened.

Gilmour traveled to Bellingham, where he met his prisoner for the first time at the Bellingham Jail. Before the meeting, he recalled the words of Dankworth in a training session — "Any interrogator worth his salt can put himself in the place of the suspect."

After shaking hands with Mayo, Gilmour spent twenty minutes getting acquainted and reading the prisoner his rights while explaining them in a friendly and supportive manner, suggesting by his words and tone that he understood how Mayo must feel under the circumstances. Eventually the conversation got around to Mayo's story, which the prisoner was by then anxious to tell.

After leaving the prison farm, Mayo had been hitch-hiking when Zimmerman and Paul drove up, stopped, and offered him a ride. The three hit it off. Zimmerman was an affable man and talked constantly about rocks, his beloved hobby. Since Mayo seemed not to be in a

hurry, they stopped at Sheep Mountain to look for interesting rocks. When they drove on, Zimmerman re-
minded Mayo that their destination was Gunsight
Mountain Lodge.

Mayo began to worry about his ride coming to an
end. He didn't want to hitchhike again, fearing he
might be captured. When they neared Jackass Creek,
Mayo said he needed to take a leak and wondered if
they would mind stopping for a few minutes.
Zimmerman drove down a side road and they all left
the Land Cruiser, hiking over to the creek.

When they were well out of sight of the highway,
Mayo told the trooper, he started to feel strange and
warm inside "like I was loaded on marijuana." Mayo
said he felt like he was reading their minds and they
were reading his. He said he "started thinking funny . .
. like they were inviting me to do what I did."

When Larry Zimmerman leaned over to pick up a
small rock, Mayo picked up another rock, a large one,
and smashed it on the man's head. He then turned to
the petrified boy and said, "sorry kid." He smashed another rock against Paul Hair's skull. He took a wallet
and keys from the dead man's pockets and drove away
in the Toyota. He said he was confused and didn't understand why Zimmerman and the boy weren't beside
him, but he drove on, his mind reeling.

Mayo said he drove to Fairbanks, where the Land
Cruiser ran out of gas. A police officer came by and
offered to take him to a service station. Mayo was certain he would be arrested, but went along and bought
gas with Zimmerman's money. Later, he went in search
of a buyer for several of Zimmerman's guns that he
found in the vehicle. Mayo sold the guns on the street
and used the money to fly to Anchorage, where he bur-
glarized a home to raise more cash before flying on to
California. There he committed yet another burglary,

stole another car, then drove to Portland to see his mother.

Willis Mayo's confession to Sergeant Gilmour became part of the official record and was presented in his trial the following May. In a one-day proceeding, a judge ruled him not guilty by reason of insanity, ordering his confinement to a maximum-security institution for the criminally insane in California. State troopers said Mayo was released a few years later when psychiatrists decided he had overcome his mental problems and was ready to return to society. He apparently never returned to Alaska.

chapter six

The Search for Yellow 39

Gloria Hibbs hated her husband working as a night cabbie, picking up drunks, whores, and low lifes. But it was a way to get by until he could land a pipeline job.

Andrew Dolchok's life was a mess. Sexually, he was confused. He heard voices. Some called him Andrew; some called him Andrea. At age twenty-seven, he had been arrested twenty-six times. Anchorage police considered him a one-man crime wave.

His offenses included rape, burglary, and being drunk in public. On July 7, 1971, Dolchok was in jail again, this time for forging a stolen check. In a quaint custom of the time, after he paid a seventy-five dollar fine for being drunk in public, the judge gave him a twenty-four-hour pass from jail to go back on the street and raise one thousand dollars to bail himself out on the forgery charge.

The likelihood that Dolchok could raise one thousand dollars legally was remote. More likely the judge was hoping the prisoner would just leave town.

Andrew Dolchok did try to raise money but didn't intend to post bail with it. He returned to his old haunts on Fourth Avenue where he broke into a car to steal a jacket lying on the seat. He found cash in one of the jacket pockets, but the special prize was a .32 semi-automatic pistol he found hidden underneath it.

Dolchok drank his way through the cash, then dragged a woman into an abandoned building and raped her. Afterward, he headed back to the bars and tried to cadge free drinks from bartenders and their customers.

When no drinks were forthcoming, he asked those with familiar faces to loan him money. The bartenders threw him out on the street. There, he propositioned a prostitute, hoping for free sex, but she wanted cash in advance.

The unending rejections compounded his anger. After he was thrown out of a Fourth Avenue bar, he stepped back into the bar briefly to call a taxi. The bartender and his customers watched in relief as Yellow Cab #39 picked up Dolchok and drove away. The driver, Harry Hibbs, forty-eight, called his dispatcher indicating he had picked up a passenger who wanted to go to Eagle River — a large fare if the passengers actually had the money. Hibbs hoped Dolchok was telling the truth when he said he was headed for a friend's house and could get money there for the fare. A more experienced cabbie would have demanded his money before leaving Fourth Avenue, but Hibbs was new at his job.

A much-decorated veteran of World War II and the Korean Conflict, Harry Hibbs had been in Alaska just six weeks, arriving from Chicago with his wife and three-year-old son. They moved to the state to be near his wife's family and to position them selves to get work building the trans-Alaska pipeline. In the meantime, Hibbs was driving a Yellow Cab owned by his brother-in-law.

Once out on the Glenn Highway, Andrew Dolchok pulled out the pistol and ordered Hibbs to drive past Eagle River to Birchwood Loop Road. The taxi driver tried to signal that he had a problem by speeding up behind and past another vehicle. The other driver grew angry, chased the cab, and wrote down its number but didn't call anyone.

When Yellow Cab #39 reached Birchwood Loop, Dolchok directed Hibbs to a remote area, where he ordered him to get out of the car and beg for his life — on his knees. The stunned driver gave Dolchok his wallet and emptied out his pockets, handing over a total of eighty-one dollars in cash. Dolchok had expected more and demanded it. Hibbs said he had no more money and was pleading for his life when Dolchok put the pistol behind the driver's ear and pulled the trigger. When the man fell, Dolchok shot him one more time for good measure, this time through the side of his chest, into his heart.

He took Hibbs' watch and a pair of sunglasses that he thought looked cool. He grabbed the driver's dead arms and dragged the body twenty feet into some nearby brush, pulling it along with the feet, shoes and pants dangling behind. He covered the remains with brush and drove off. Worried that he would be arrested, Dolchok emptied Hibbs' wallet, threw it out the car window, then drove the taxi past Palmer to Chickaloon where he drove the vehicle into the Chickaloon River. He went through the cab carefully, wiping every surface to remove his fingerprints. Finally he waded ashore and walked away, leaving the vehicle in a section of river overhung by thick trees.

Dolchok walked several miles to the home of Johnny Luster, one of Alaska's most colorful characters and a former neighbor. Luster had come from Montana to be a guide and outfitter. He ran a string of saddle and packhorses to take grizzly-bear hunters up into the Chickaloon Mountains, to the headwaters of the river, where the big bears roamed. Dolchok had known Johnny Luster for many years. Luster knew Dolchok only too well.

Dolchok arrived at the Luster homestead about 5:30 A.M., smelling of alcohol, his arms covered with scratches, and shivering despite the relative warmth of the July morning. He told Luster that he wanted to rent a few horses to take him up into the mountains. The guide served Dolchok breakfast but did so uneasily, remembering the time when Dolchok killed Luster's wife's dog by smashing its head with a two-by-four. The dog had barked when Dolchok tried to climb through a window into the Luster family home. His temper flared and he walked back to the chained animal with a board and silenced it forever.

Luster had hired Dolchok for a time as an assistant guide, but then on a hunt, Luster left his clients in camp while he shot a moose for camp meat. After downing the moose, he slipped his rifle back into its saddle scabbard, climbed down from his horse, and approached the dead animal with a skinning knife. He expected Dolchok to help, but when turned back, his assistant was pointing a rifle at him.

"If you kill me," Luster said, "you'll have to kill everyone in camp." Dolchok lowered the rifle. He never worked for the guide again.

That morning in 1971, while he was eating the breakfast placed before him, Luster's wife entered the kitchen and was shocked to see Andrew Dolchok at her table. The Luster family wanted nothing more to do with the strange young man and, as soon as they could, sent him on his way — without horses. He last was seen walking up the rough road leading from the homestead.

Andrew Dolchok's sister and brother-in-law lived in Palmer. Hitchhiking to the little Matanuska Valley town, he told the couple he had been released from jail with no cash and needed a room and some clothes. They were cautious, knowing of Dolchok's often-bizarre behavior. They drove him to a hotel, gave him a little cash, and directed him to a store where he bought fresh clothes. At the hotel, Dolchok strayed into the bar, got drunk, left to burglarize a nearby building, and brought two young girls back to his room. He guessed their ages at thirteen. He had sex with both girls and sent them on their way.

The taxi dispatcher grew worried when Yellow 39 stopped answering his radio. In his short time with the company, Harry Hibbs had shown himself to be a trustworthy driver, and it seemed unlike him to disappear during working hours. The dispatcher called the driver's home to see if he was taking a break there or had quit early without calling in. The early-morning call terrified Gloria Hibbs. She hated the idea that her husband was working all night, picking up drunks, whores, and who-knows-what down on Fourth Avenue. But it was a way for her husband to make a living until he could land a pipeline job. Mrs. Hibbs called police to report Harry missing, setting off an official search. The taxi office sent out a radio bulletin asking all drivers to watch for Yellow 39.

Investigators went to the Fourth Avenue bar. Had anyone seen the passenger who called for a cab about 1:30 A.M.? The club's owner said he had seen a twenty-something Alaska Native man at the bar harassing his bartender and customers. The bar owner didn't know the man's name, but he had seen the man occasionally and considered him to be a nuisance.

The Yellow Cab managers were convinced that Harry Hibbs was a victim of foul play. The reported behavior of the driver's last-known passenger was disturbing. An intensive search involving patrol cars, taxis, and state troopers in aircraft turned up nothing. Then, on Sunday, a searcher found Harry's empty wallet beside the Glenn Highway, three miles from Palmer.

Because Yellow 39 last was seen in downtown Anchorage and the driver reported he was heading for Eagle River, Anchorage police and troopers worked together on the case. The investigative team visited bars and restaurants. A police artist met with the bartender and customers at the last bar Dolchok visited and created a sketch of Yellow 39's last fare. The sketch was sent to police agencies and to customs officers at the U.S.-Canada border and distributed to news media and shown to bartenders and customers in Anchorage drinking spots. Newspapers throughout the region published the sketch. Taxi drivers posted it in their cars. Some drivers were angry, some were fearful, and many took to carrying pistols. Almost all carried flashlights loaded with Mace spray.

On Monday, two children playing in a wooded area off Birchwood Loop Road stumbled across the driver's brush-covered corpse and ran home screaming. Squad cars rushed to the scene with sirens wailing and lights flashing.

Lieutenant Tom Anderson and Sergeant Don Church of the trooper's Criminal Investigation Bureau staked

out the area as a crime scene. They made notes on Harry Hibbs's wounds, his out-turned pockets, the mud on the knees of his pants and the backs of his heels, and drag marks on the ground leading up to the body. They noted with disgust that the victim appeared to have been on his knees when the killer shot him in the back of the head. Both bullets passed through his body, so the officers had no slugs for comparison to the original weapon, if it could be found. They did find a mud-covered shoe and two empty bullet casings.

The aerial search for the missing taxi, grounded for lack of results, was renewed. Flying eyes peered down, trying to penetrate the dense forest and undergrowth in a wide circle around the scene and nearby roads. Police put a dozen patrol cars into the ground search and Yellow Cab drivers joined the effort. Troopers asked hunters, fishermen, and campers to watch for an abandoned yellow 1970 Dodge taxi with the number thirty-nine on its doors.

Harry Hibbs was buried in an American Legion ceremony, just three days before what would have been his forty-ninth birthday. His wife, son, other family members, cab drivers, and friends winced as the rifles fired in the traditional military salute. They fought back tears as a bugler played Taps, saying their final goodbyes and turning away, their hearts heavy. The murdered cab driver was laid to rest in the Veterans Garden of Anchorage Memorial Park.

Two hours after the funeral, a borough appraiser sent to estimate the value of a lodge under construction on the Chickaloon River wandered to the back of the property and pushed through a thick patch of trees to look at the river. There, in a foot of water and under a canopy of foliage, he found Yellow 39.

Investigators hurried to the scene followed by the troopers' rolling crime lab. A thorough search was made, but the vehicle yielded few useful clues. Despite wide circulation of the artist's sketch and dozens of tips, detectives still did not know the suspect's name.

However, when Johnny Luster heard that the missing taxi had been found near his homestead, he called troopers and told them about his experience with Andrew Dolchok.

Dolchok's unabated anger and lack of good sense kept him from going to ground. Instead, he got into trouble again. He was arrested on July 13 in Fairbanks, the day after Harry Hibbs's body was found, and charged with drunkenness, resisting arrest, and joyriding.

Fairbanks Police Lieutenant Lonnie McClung noticed that the new prisoner in his lockup looked a lot like the sketch of the suspect in the Anchorage murder case. When arrested, Andrew had been carrying a pair of prescription sunglasses. McClung handed Dolchok the glasses and asked him to read a paragraph with them on. The prisoner couldn't read with the glasses; they were not his. A check on the prescription showed they belonged to Harry Hibbs.

McClung called state troopers, who got a grand jury indictment charging Dolchok with robbery and first-degree murder. Dolchok was rearrested in his Fairbanks cell. While awaiting return to Anchorage, Dolchok grew anxious to talk about the murder. When a fellow prisoner asked him why he was in jail, Dolchok answered, "I killed a cab driver." He told the inmate about shoot-

ing Hibbs twice and claimed that he pocketed three thousand dollars in the robbery.

Detective Church caught a Wien Air Alaska flight
to Fairbanks, picked up Dolchok at the Fairbanks jail,
and caught the next plane back to Anchorage with his
prisoner in handcuffs.

When Church and Dolchok arrived at Anchorage
International Airport, a throng of media awaited them.
Church led his prisoner protectively through the crowd
and pushed him into a patrol car.

Church had tried to put Dolchok at ease and talked
to him like a friend, even stopping to buy him cigarettes
on the drive from the Anchorage airport to the state
lockup. Dolchok was terrified, but impressed by
Church's kindness. When the trooper offered to stop
for a cup of coffee, Dolchok jumped at the chance. Inside the restaurant, Church was careful not to ask the
prisoner any questions about the murder and specifi-
cally told him that he didn't intend to talk about the
case. Dolchok said he wanted to talk and volunteered
the whole story, from start to finish. He told Church
that he had pawned the cab driver's watch in Fairbanks
and threw the pistol away in a swamp near the murder
site. When Church asked if Dolchok would tell him the
complete story again for the record, Dolchok agreed.
Back at trooper headquarters, Detective Don Church
typed while Andrew Dolchok dictated. Afterward, the
prisoner signed the confession.

"I typed it exactly as he told it," Church said.
"This was the amazing thing. *I never asked any questions!*"

Troopers returned to the crime scene with a metal
detector looking for the murder weapon. No luck. Neither did they find the prostitute whom Dolchok solic-
ited hours before the robbery or the teenagers with
whom he had sex at the Palmer hotel.

Andrew Dolchok confessed to the rape he committed the night of the murder, then asked to be turned
over to Anchorage police on that charge, apparently
hoping that the revolving door he encountered earlier
at the jail would free him again. Both police agencies
were frustrated that the courts had allowed Dolchok to
return to the street after twenty-six arrests. There would
be no release this time. The judge's earlier hope that
Dolchok would leave town had been in vain and many
people suffered for it, especially Harry Hibbs and his
family.

At his trial the following year, Andrew Dolchok
waived a jury trial. His court-appointed lawyer said the
killer couldn't help himself — the young man was mentally ill and wanted to be committed to a mental hospital.
He said his client's father was convicted of murder before
him, and that Dolchok was angry about his sexual con-
fusion. The defense lawyer said despite Dolchok's rape of
an unknown number of women and statutory rape of
the two girls in Palmer, the troubled young man was homosexual. The lawyer claimed Dolchok had two personalities and went by two names, Andrew and Andrea. A
psychiatrist testified that Dolchok was schizophrenic and
paranoid, but competent enough to stand trial.

The judge ruled that although Dolchok was mentally disturbed, his actions before and after the murder
showed he had substantial capacity to control his behavior. The judge found him guilty, gave him a life sentence, and ordered him sent to a federal facility for treatment of the criminally insane in Springfield, Illinois. *The
Anchorage Times* congratulated the judge for his finding in the cab driver's murder, calling Andrew Dolchok
"one of the most brutal, cold-blooded murderers of recent years."

Dolchok asked for a retrial in 1974, saying that he
thought Trooper Sergeant Church — because of his

name — was a priest, which was why he confessed. At the hearing, with Church on the stand, Dolchok's lawyer argued that the detective couldn't prove his claim that Hibbs was on his knees when he was shot. Church reached into his evidence bag and pulled out the murder victim's pants. The knees were still covered with dried mud. The appeal was denied.

Dolchok later appealed a second time and was denied once more. Dolchok showed up at that hearing in full-drag costume, including a wig, women's clothes, and lipstick. He had apparently settled on the Andrea personality and was then serving his time in an Arizona prison facility, where he remains.

chapter seven

A Fairbanks Divorce

The murder suspect, a convicted felon, told troopers he had borrowed the .22 pistol to go rabbit hunting then went to a movie instead. But he couldn't account for seven missing cartridges.

Verna Hofhines stepped from a taxi, pulled her fur parka tight, and scurried up the icy walk to her trailer home in the Fairbanks suburb of College. It was 40 below early on a January morning in 1972. The trailer door was open to the cold and lights were blazing. Inside, Vera Hofhines found her twenty-two-year-old husband, Buck, sprawled on the floor. She later told police that at first she thought he might have fallen asleep, but around him lay a pool of blood. And scattered in the already-thickened blood were empty bullet cartridges.

When investigators arrived, they counted the bullet holes and determined that that Buck Hofhines, a helicopter mechanic at nearby Fort Wainwright, had been shot seven times, virtually each one a fatal shot. The shell casings were ejected from a .22 automatic. Hofhines had bullet holes in his forehead and chest, and five in the base of his skull. State Trooper Rollie Port turned to Verna and said, "Lady, somebody wanted to make damn sure your husband was dead."

The attractive young bride, a dancer at the Gold Rush Saloon, told the trooper that she had found her husband upon her returned from a night of bumps and grinds. It was to have been her scheduled night off, but she was asked to fill in for a friend at the Flame Room. Buck hadn't wanted her to go, but she had committed herself. Besides, she and Buck could use the money.

Verna Hofhines had visited the Flame Room early that evening on one of her sideline ventures, working for Fairbanks Police making drug buys with an undercover officer. Verna had dinner with Buck when he came home from Fort Wainwright about 5:30 P.M., then left the house in their pickup truck at hour later to meet officer Jimmy Clements at police headquarters. Clements dressed in his undercover clothes, put on a wig, and they drove together to the Flame Room, where they nursed drinks and tried to make a drug buy.

The undercover drug operation was unsuccessful that night, but the Flame's manager spotted Verna and asked her to fill in for a sick dancer. She agreed but said she had to go home first, to tell her husband and to check on her seven-month-old son. At home, Buck insisted she take a cab to work fearing the pickup would not start in the sub-zero weather when she finished work. Verna spent the evening dancing and occasionally showing the customers a little flesh. The drinkers expressed their appreciation by buying rounds, filling the till, and keeping the manager happy.

Troopers decided there was something unusual about the murder scene. There was no sign of a struggle or forced entry. Hofhines's' wallet was still in his pocket, his small amount of cash untouched. Nothing was missing from the trailer. Trooper Port asked Verna if she had any former boyfriends who might have been jealous enough to shoot her husband. She shook her head. They had been married a month and had known one another only a month before that. She didn't know much about his background. They had met at the Gold Rush. Buck Hofhines seemed lonely and depressed. He had enlisted in the Army in Idaho. He was unhappy working at the subarctic base and talked frequently about going back home to Idaho.

"I guess we got married because we felt sorry for each other," she said. "He wanted me to quit work, but he didn't make enough with his Army pay for us to live on."

Verna Hofhines said she and her husband never had been threatened, and she didn't think anybody knew about her work with Officer Clements, who told Trooper Port that the drug connection was an unlikely reason for the murder. He and Verna had caught a few small narcotics pushers but never came close to any of the major operators in the city. Verna said she had no idea whether Buck might have enemies of his own.

State troopers sealed the trailer until crime scene specialists could fly up from Anchorage. Troopers canvassed the neighborhood but found only a college student who remembered hearing some popping sounds about 9:00 the night before. None of the neighbors knew the young couple and none recalled seeing visitors.

Because Buck Hofhines's wounds suggested an execution-style murder, nine troopers were assigned full-time to the case, including the crime scene investigators. Trooper Claude Swackhammer was put in charge. The trailer was dusted for fingerprints. The body and blood pool, empty cartridge casings, the floor and furniture nearby were photographed. Investigators determined that the bullets fired into the victim's forehead and chest came from a distance, but those in the back of his head were fired with the gun held close against the base of his skull. That suggested the killer had walked into the trailer, put the soldier down with two shots straight-on, then had come in close and pumped five more into the back of his head.

The investigation went on around the clock. After two days, trooper Swackhammer reported to his supervisor, Corporal John Lucking, that his team had found no clues pointing to a murderer. Obviously it was not a random killing, he said, "but don't ask me why. We haven't the foggiest idea of why he was killed."

The investigators checked passenger manifests for outgoing flights and learned that a cab driver had flown to Seattle the night of the murder. Ed Brown was twenty-two, handsome, and lonely. He had quit his job without notice the day after the murder. Brown's trip logs showed he supposedly had been at a cabstand in downtown Fairbanks from 9 P.M. until 10:30 P.M. Friday night, about the time of the murder, though the dispatcher had tried to call him on the radio about 9:45 without response. Brown's trip log for a previous Tuesday showed he had reported a breakdown and was out of service for ninety minutes near the Hofhines' trailer. The company president said "breakdowns" often occurred when a driver wanted to visit one of the women he met in his work. Brown's roommate said he was surprised by the taxi driver's sudden and unannounced departure.

Swackhammer's team asked police in Seattle and in Brown's hometown of Madera, California, to watch for him. They also dispatched a surveillance team to watch Verna Hofhines when she accompanied her husband's body to Idaho for burial. Troopers wanted to know if she met with anyone matching Brown's description along the way.

The hope that the cab driver might prove to be their murderer was a bit of a long shot, but it was the only real lead in the case. Then, something happened that made them forget about Ed Brown. Swackhammer got an anonymous telephone tip suggesting that he "ask Steve Carlin about his .22 automatic, and who had it on the Friday night that Buck Hofhines was killed." The man hung up before the trooper could trace the call. But investigators quickly found and interviewed Steve Carlin, who confirmed that he owned a .22 automatic and turned over the pistol. He told troopers that an acquaintance, Dennis Anthony, had borrowed the weapon on the Friday of the shooting to go rabbit hunting.

The troopers knew Dennis Anthony, twenty-nine, a longhaired harmonica player who hung out at the Gold Rush. Anthony had a criminal record, having served six years in prison for the armed robbery of an Anchorage Safeway store in March 1966.

Carlin said when he gave Anthony the automatic it was loaded with a full nine-round clip. He said Anthony brought the gun back at 2 A.M. the next morning. Anthony told Carlin he hadn't used the pistol, having decided to take his girlfriend to the movies rather than go hunting.

"When he returned the weapon he asked me to say he had borrowed a rifle, in case anybody asked," Carlin said. Anthony told him he was worried that he might be arrested for being a felon in possession of a handgun.

"How many cartridges were in the clip when he returned it?" Swackhammer asked.

"Two."

Troopers sent Steve Carlin's .22 automatic and spent cartridges found at the crime scene for ballistics comparison at a FBI crime laboratory. Knowing that it might be a few weeks before the results came back, investigators worried that Dennis Anthony might hear about their visit to Carlin and leave town. They approached District Attorney Monroe Clayton in search of a way to interrogate Anthony without the ballistics evidence. Clayton said they were in luck. The U.S. Attorney's office in Anchorage had just notified him that it was seeking a federal indictment against Anthony for attempting to purchase a handgun the previous November. He had used a false name and identification.

Clayton issued a warrant for Anthony's arrest, which would allow troopers to hold him until results of the ballistics test came back. They arrested Anthony the day Verna Hofhines returned from her husband's funeral in Idaho. The detectives still had no motive, but they were beginning to suspect that the brief marriage of Buck and Verna Hofhines might have been uphappy. The women at the Gold Rush said Verna often complained about her husband — and seemed bitter. The couple frequently quarreled about her job, and he accused her of meeting other men in the afternoons, when he was on duty at the Army post.

The officers also learned that Verna knew Dennis Anthony, although any romance between them seemed unlikely. Anthony was engaged to Helen Goodley and planned to marry her as soon as he got a steady job. The only motive troopers could think of was that Verna might have wanted her husband dead so she could collect his ten thousand dollars in GI insurance.

Under questioning, Anthony admitted that he borrowed Carlin's pistol but claimed he never used it. He said he left it under his car seat while he took Helen to a movie and visited a few bars. Anthony maintained he was with Helen all night except for about ten minutes when he left the theater to warm up the car. He said he never counted the bullets in the clip and had given the gun back to Carlin just as he borrowed it.

The FBI report showed that Carlin's automatic was the murder weapon, but both of Swackhammer's prime suspects had alibis. Verna Hofhines had been highly visible throughout the evening on stage at the Flame Room. Dennis Anthony's fiancé and other witnesses confirmed he was in a theater and in several bars about at the same time.

Nonetheless, the district attorney filed first-degree murder charges against the pair. Their lawyers ridiculed the charges and said it was impossible for their clients to be in two places at the same time. Verna's lawyer added that it was "unthinkable that the bride of less than a month could have plotted the death of her husband."

At the preliminary hearing, a judge ruled that there was insufficient evidence to hold Anthony, ordering him released. Verna Hofhines was ordered held for trial. When the judge left the courtroom, Verna stood in a side aisle with her parents, weeping, and asked reporters, "How could anyone even think such a horrible thing, let alone believe it?"

Monroe Clayton was convinced that evidence against Anthony was strong and would hold up, and that the hearing judge was wrong. The district attorney filed the charges a second time and a joint trial was scheduled for the two defendants. The story received major coverage from news media. Anthony told reporters that the state troopers were persecuting him because of his prior record. "I made one mistake six years ago," he said, "and they want me to keep paying it for the rest of my life."

The trial opened on June 16, 1972 with a packed courtroom, jammed courthouse hallways, and more people waiting outside. Regulars in the downtown Fairbanks bars wagered on the chances of acquittals. An apparently confident Anthony told his fellow drinkers that alibi witnesses would sink the state's case, that nobody could place him at the murder scene. The harmonica player's long hair was now gone. Dennis Anthony looked neat and wholesome for the first time in many years. He wore a tie and jacket, resembling a young college professor. He was ready to face the jury.

Buck Hofhines's widow wore a plain dress buttoned to the neck and glasses, and her dark hair was pulled back in a bun. She looked like a schoolteacher. When the Superior Court convened at 10 A.M., Verna's lawyer announced that his client would like to change her plea.

Judge Everett Hepp turned to Verna and asked how she wished to plead.

"Guilty, your honor."

Anthony's eyes and mouth went wide, as did his lawyer's. The large audience was shocked and a buzz ran through the room, prompting the judge to bang his gavel and call for order. Various legalities took up the balance of the day. When Verna was called to the stand the next morning, she said in a low and meek voice that her marriage to Buck Hohfines was a bad idea and went sour shortly after the wedding. They argued about her dancing, she said, and "he slapped me around a lot." The night before he was killed, he tore off her nightgown, twisted her arm, and punched her several times.

The young dancer said she had known Dennis Anthony for about six months, and knew that he recently was released from prison. About a week before the murder she ran into him at the Flame Lounge. The district attorney asked what they talked about.

"I asked him if he knew of anyone that could do a specific job for me."

How did Anthony respond?

"He said he probably did," Verna testified. "He asked what kind of job was it. I said it wasn't a pleasant job, that I wanted to be a widow."

To another question from the district attorney, Verna said: "He asked me how much I was willing to pay for it. I said I didn't have any money at the present time, but I could get hold of about five thousand dollars. He said he did know of someone who could do the job for me and when did I want it done?"

"What did you say?" she was asked.

"I told him as soon as possible and he said it would be done before the weekend was over."

"When was the money to be paid?"

"After settlement of the insurance."

Verna said she described her husband for Anthony and gave him directions to their trailer. But the murder almost went awry when the contract killer showed up at the trailer on Friday at 5:30, before Buck came home. Her husband drove up as Verna and Anthony were talking at the trailer door. Anthony left, telling her to tell her husband he had come to check the lights.

Verna headed for Fairbanks Police headquarters shortly afterward, met Officer Clements, and went to the Flame Room looking for drug dealers. When the club manager asked her to dance that night, she left, saying she had to tell her husband and check on her baby. She admitted in court that she thought the shooting might already have taken place and she didn't want to leave the baby alone too long. Instead, she found her husband taking a nap on the couch. He awoke and they had a brief, nasty conversation before she headed back to the Flame Room five minutes later.

About midnight, Anthony came into the club and called her over. He told Vera she was a widow. She went back to dancing until 2:30 A.M., when she headed for home.

Verna ran into Anthony in a restaurant on First Avenue shortly after he was arrested on the felon-in-possession charge. He was unfriendly, claimed he didn't know her or her husband, and didn't want to have anything to do with her. She said she was sorry the police had given him such a hard time.

The next time she saw him was at the booking desk when they were arrested. They had a chance to speak briefly and Anthony said if they both had kept their mouths shut, the district attorney wouldn't have a case against either one of them.

Cross-examined by Anthony's lawyer, Verna said she changed her plea to guilty because her conscience was bothering her. She said that the murder might never have happened if a contract killer had not been available to her.

"I didn't do the actual shooting," she said. "I just more or less arranged for it, and I just frankly don't want to stand alone in this thing."

Later, when the lawyer pressed her, Verna admitted that her conscience was less a factor than the reduced six-year sentence the district attorney had offered in exchange for her testimony against Anthony.

Dennis Anthony did not testify on his own behalf, but his lawyer presented several alibi witnesses who placed him far from the Hofhines trailer. He argued that although his client had the murder weapon in his possession and returned it with seven bullets missing, he could not have been in two places at one time. He argued that a third person might have done the shooting and suggested that Verna herself had pulled the trigger after Anthony gave her the pistol. He claimed Anthony was keeping silent to protect her. He suggested it also was possible that an unknown third person had committed the murder.

The district attorney countered that if a third party was the real shooter, then Anthony had to be the one who hired the killer and would be able to identify him. If that were the case, he said, Anthony could get the same deal that Verna Hofhines got — six years in exchange for testimony against the real killer. No such testimony was offered.

Dennis Anthony was found guilty of murder in the first degree and sentenced to life in prison. While there, he submitted a long series of appeals and corresponded often with news media about his life of persecution by the legal system.

Anthony was an increasingly surly and difficult prisoner. In 1974, he escaped from Eagle River Correctional Institution near Anchorage. During his brief freedom, he went to the home of a guard whom he hated and raped the man's wife. After his recapture, he was imprisoned for a time outside Alaska, and then in 1988 was returned to a maximum-security facility at Seward. He died there two years later, his life and career of violence ended by cancer.

Verna Hofhines served her sentence in a federal prison outside Alaska and afterward started a new life in a community elsewhere on the West Coast.

chapter eight
Alaska's Billy the Kid

Getting acquainted over a friendly cup of coffee, trooper investigator Jim Vaden predicted to the cold-blooded murder that he would be killed in a shootout with police or killed by "friends."

Gary Zieger's first known murder came to light when a young man told his girlfriend that he knew about a fatal shooting that occurred in 1970. She refused to marry him unless he told his story to police. So, he called state troopers and told them he had been riding around with Zieger in Zieger's truck six months earlier. They had stopped to pick up a young hitchhiker and drove to a secluded spot. Zieger borrowed his friend's gun, held it to the stranger's head, and ordered the man to perform oral sex. After the encounter, Zieger shot the hitchhiker and threw his body over an embankment at the Anchorage dump. The body was found the next day, but there were no suspects or investigative leads, so the murder was listed as unsolved.

After the witness called, troopers sent an officer to the man's apartment to collect the gun, but the trooper had to wait for a search warrant. Before the warrant arrived, Zieger showed up, entered the apartment and left. When the search finally was conducted, the pistol could not be found.

The investigators went to the spot where the body had been thrown and used a metal detector to find empty cartridges from a 9mm pistol. The shells had lain there for six months. Examining the weapon's unique markings, called lands and grooves, which could be used as evidence if the weapon could be located.

Zieger never was prosecuted. The witness's word and the empty cartridges were not enough to make a case.

Two days before Christmas 1971, pretty Celia van Zanten, an eighteen-year-old student, left her home in Turnagain to walk to a store. She never got there. On Christmas Day, the young woman's body was found near McHugh Creek Campground south of Anchorage. Van Zanten had been gagged and raped. Evidence at the scene indicated she was alive after being thrown into a ravine, and tried to climb out, but with her hands tied behind her, she repeatedly fell and slowly froze to death.

Two months later, eighteen-year-old Shirley Ann Jones left an Anchorage nightclub with an unidentified man and was found the next morning in a truck yard on the east side of town. Raped and beaten, she was near death from exposure. The woman never regained consciousness.

The following August, Zingre "ZeZe" Mason, an attractive twenty-year-old airport employee, left her Sand Lake home to retrieve her car from a repair shop. Her friends had advised her against hitchhiking, but she was an adventurous young woman with a rebellious streak. She put aside her inhibitions, stepped to the side of the road, and stuck out her thumb. Mason failed to show up for work the next day. Her worried parents called the repair shop and were told her car had not been claimed.

Six days later, children playing in the remote part of a gravel pit near the intersection of Sand Lake Road and Dimond Boulevard stumbled across a woman's body. They ran shrieking for help. Arriving state troopers found the dead ZeZe Mason hidden under a tree, naked from the waist down, just a few miles from her home.

Investigators were enraged and vowed to find the killer. Sergeant Walter Gilmour of the Trooper's Criminal Investigation Bureau took charge of the case. Because there was no sure sign where the slaying occurred, the Anchorage Police Department sent an officer to join the team. The detectives asked for information from the public but were not optimistic. Nothing useful had come in after similar appeals were made following the first two murders. Still, they were interested in anyone who might have seen a four-wheel-drive pickup near the gravel pit or a young woman getting into a truck anywhere along Mason's route to the repair shop.

Gilmour's team worked twenty hours without a break, and then cut back to sixteen-hour shifts, logging more than four hundred hours in the first three days after ZeZe Mason's body was found.

Coroner Ronnie Bray was furious. "This makes the third case I have had in eight months like this," she told a reporter. "I don't want this kind of business." The coroner said the young woman appeared to have been killed the night she disappeared. Her head and face had been beaten savagely, and the young woman was stabbed repeatedly. Death was attributed to severe head wounds and loss of blood. Detectives assumed the Mason had been raped, but the autopsy and pathology lab tests suggested that she might have engaged in consensual sex immediately before her death. Near her body and in remote portions of the gravel pit were several sets of tire tracks. Detectives suspected that among them would be imprints left by the killer's pickup truck.

Leading from the tire tracks to the body were bloodstains and drag marks suggesting that Mason had been killed elsewhere and dumped there. The tracks had a distinctive heavy tread typical of tires used by four-wheel enthusiasts for traction in mud, snow, and soft sand. Three of the tires seemed to be mounted backward. Troopers made plaster casts and added them to their modest collection of evidence. They also extended the crime scene investigation to a five-mile radius and soon found similar tracks and transmission fluid drippings at Campbell Creek, more than two miles away.

Sergeant Gilmour's team received a few promising tips. Because Mason's murder was the third in a series, and because all victims seemed to be innocents who fell in with bad company, the investigators found they had the public's full attention. One tipster, a gravel-truck driver named Hiram Matthews, reported seeing a young woman matching the victim's description climbing into a pickup with two men around the time ZeZe Mason disappeared. He said he saw the pickup again in the back of the gravel pit, near where the body later was found, but by this time it carried only two people—a man and a woman who appeared to be making out.

Another caller, Ralph Keiner, said he was riding with a co-worker, Gary Zieger, that afternoon when Zieger picked up a young woman hitchhiker. Zieger dropped Keiner off near a South Anchorage fire station. Keiner said Zieger had a large knife on the dashboard of the truck. Michael Beaver, Gary Zieger's boss at Arctic Pipelines Inc., said another employee reported seeing the Zieger washing his pickup in Campbell Creek on the day ZeZe Mason died. This was where detectives had made casts of tire tracks like those found near her body.

Then, investigators received a strange call from a woman complaining that they were persecuting her biker boyfriend; whom she said was not the murderer. Gilmour was amused. He never had heard of her boyfriend and never had known anyone to come forward with an alibi for a prospective suspect before the person became a suspect. The woman was convinced investigators were close to arresting her lover, who often drove his pickup truck in the gravel pit where the body was found. The woman said she knew who the real killer was.

Her boyfriend was a tire-shop worker who had helped a young man mount a set of all-weather tires onto a truck he often drove into the gravel pit. She said the real murderer had been mentioned in the newspaper recently in connection with a rescue from a disabled boat on Cook Inlet. The detectives checked back copies of local newspapers and found that Gary Zieger had gained brief notoriety when rescued from a boat with a blown engine.

Detectives called on the woman's boyfriend, who admitted that he and Zieger had stolen the tires and inadvertently had mounted three of them backward. Zieger decided to leave them that way rather than go to the trouble of remounting them.

Troopers got a search warrant for Zieger's truck, went to his house, and examined the pickup, pulling out and inspecting its floor mats and taking samples from inside surfaces. The truck's tires and wheelbase measurements were an exact match with a set found at the crime scene, even to the odd way the wheels were mounted. The interior had been washed clean but the officers found small amounts of what appeared to be blood, including a dime-sized smear on the inside panel of the driver's side door below the armrest.

Gary Zieger was arrested on a warrant charging him with first-degree murder, murder during an attempted rape, and murder during a robbery. The robbery charge was based on the fact that ZeZe's Mason's ring, wallet, checkbook, some clothing, and a small amount of money were missing. Zieger was lodged at the state jail and held on $75,000 bond. The detective team remained tight-lipped about its findings, but *Anchorage Daily News* quoted an unnamed source as saying that the blood in Zieger's truck appeared to be a match for ZeZe Mason's.

Although the investigation was making considerable headway, the pressures of the case and frayed nerves caused a few missteps and as a result, tempers flared. Coroner Ronnie Bray blew up when troopers gave the preliminary pathologist's report to the news media before she saw a copy. The report said Mason had massive skull fractures from blows with a blunt instrument and twelve stab wounds, including one in the chest and another that partially severed an artery in her left arm. At least three of the knife wounds and any of the skull fractures could have killed her. The inside of one thumb and several fingers contained superficial cuts indicating

that she might have tried to defend herself by grabbing the attacker's knife.

The coroner was furious about the suggestion that the victim might have engaged in consensual sex before her death.

"I have received no police report and no autopsy report," she told a reporter. "The coroner's job is to find out how a person died, and it's the troopers' job to find out who is responsible." Bray said the trooper press release "was in very bad taste and wholly unnecessary."

"I can just imagine how upset that poor girl's family is since the troopers released that information this afternoon. I just don't let things like that out of my office. One must have concern for the living as well as for the dead in a situation like this."

The detectives were chastened yet determined to make a case against Zieger and enthusiastic about the quality of the evidence they were collecting.

On September 8, Superior Court Judge C. J. Occhipinti decided he had heard enough. He ordered Zieger's lawyer, the public defender agency, the district attorney's office, the police, and the coroner to refrain from any more public comments about the case. At a bail hearing, the public defender tried to get the bond amount reduced by attacking the warrant allegations. He claimed that the evidence against Zieger was weak and circumstantial and demanded that his client be freed.

The defense lawyer would concede only that ZeZe Mason had been found dead and that a serious crime had been committed, but he argued that the evidence did not necessarily point to his client. Among the discrepancies was the fact that one witness said he saw two men pick up a young woman in a truck. The witness thought both men had dark hair. Zieger's hair was light blond. The lawyer said Zieger was a hunter and the blood found inside his truck probably was from an animal.

Sharon Gipe, secretary and bookkeeper at Arctic Pipelines, testified that Zieger had worked for the fuel line company for a year and was a responsible, dependable, and careful employee. She said her faith in him prompted her to co-sign for his truck loan when his parents wouldn't, or couldn't, accept the financial responsibility. Gipe added that Arctic Pipelines operated the gravel pit, and that Zieger's job required him to drive through the area almost every day.

The judge was not impressed. Zieger went back to jail and stayed there, waiting for his day in court.

Investigators heard different opinions about young Zieger from friends and fellow workers. Unlike the older bookkeeper, those his age said they considered Zieger to be dangerous and violent. He was quick to anger, untrustworthy, and possibly dangerous. He had a reputation for enjoying violent sex and forcing himself on reluctant women — and sometimes men. Still, the defendant had only a minor criminal record that included one conviction for assault and battery.

Gary Zieger's murder trial opened in late January at a courthouse in Kodiak, the fishing community on an island two hundred miles southwest of Anchorage. A judge ordered it moved there in hopes of selecting a jury unbiased by extensive coverage in the Anchorage media and the controversial disclosure by troopers that ZeZe Mason may have had voluntary sex before she was killed. To make sure the jury of eight men and four women was not prejudiced by rumors or news coverage, jurors were sequestered at a local hotel.

One Kodiak resident told a reporter that island people were unlikely to be biased by what the Anchorage newspapers reported. "Most folks here tend to not believe things unless they see them," he said. "We're pretty isolated here."

Early in the trial, Zieger's new defense lawyer, Jon Larson, said that Zieger did pick up a young woman on the day of ZeZe Mason's murder, and did drive around with her, but that he dropped her off later and was occupied with other matters the rest of the day. The lawyer said it was unclear whether the young woman was Mason. Ralph Keiner, Zieger's co-worker who reported being with Zieger when he picked up a young woman hitchhiker, looked at photographs of Mason and said he couldn't be sure whether that was the young woman who climbed into the truck.

Tests showed that the substance on the truck's door panel was indeed blood, but with DNA tests still years in the future, it could not be matched to the dead woman. Other bloodstains were found on the armrest, kick panel, window on the passenger's side of the vehicle, and on a yellow hardhat found in the truck. One of the state's expert witnesses said he could only be certain that one spot of blood came from a human being; the rest came from a human or other high primate, though the likelihood that an ape had been bleeding in Gary Zieger's pickup was remote. A pathologist who studied a sample said he was not able to determine either the blood type or the sex of the person it from whom it came, nor could he say how long it had been in the truck. One specimen appeared to have been there a year, he said, but he couldn't tell about the others.

Among other evidence submitted were the wheels and tires from Zieger's truck and the plaster casts of the tire tracks found in the gravel pit. The prosecution's case took a hit when an FBI forensic specialist said the tread design on Zieger's tires was similar to that in the plaster casts but — despite the unique mismatched mounting — he couldn't be certain the same tires made both the tracks and the plastic casts.

Prosecutors planned to submit a statement given to troopers and signed by Michael Beaver, Zieger's boss, saying that Ralph Keiner told him he saw Zieger washing his truck in Campbell Creek the day of the murder. But Keiner denied telling Beaver or anybody else about seeing Zieger at Campbell Creek. Beaver then undermined his own statement, saying it might not have been true.

Assistant District Attorney William Mackey called twenty-six witnesses during five days of testimony and presented one hundred five exhibits. Yet, without evidence directly tying Zieger to the murder, the state's case was vulnerable, especially as to changing stories and conflicting accounts by witnesses. And the defense was able to bring more such witnesses to the courtroom. Three said they saw ZeZe Mason alive hours after she was seen climbing into Zieger's truck, and one woman said she gave Mason a ride between 5 and 6 P.M. that day. A storeowner said the young woman was in his shop with two other men when he closed for the night. Although the rebuttal testimony didn't rule out the possibility that Gary had killed the young woman, it did suggest that ZeZe Mason may not have been in his company continuously after truck driver Hiram Matthews saw her get into Zieger's pickup.

On the sixth day of the trial, Zieger took the stand. His lawyer asked him flatly: "Did you kill ZeZe Mason, Gary?"

The courtroom fell silent. Zieger answered in a firm, quiet voice, "No, I did not."

The prosecutor showed Zieger color photos of Mason's body. Later, he told a reporter, "I'm sorry it happened, but I'm a lot sorrier that I was arrested."

The trial ended on the ninth day. The jury deliberated for six hours, returned to the courtroom, and took their seats. The foreman read the verdict – not guilty on all three counts.

Zieger slumped in his chair in relieved exhaustion. The judge declared the case concluded and Zieger's parents rushed to the defense table for tearful hugs, handshakes, and congratulations.

In a custom of the time, newspaper headlines declared Zieger was found "innocent," which was hardly true. There is no such finding as innocent. More accurately, police and prosecutors were unable to prove that he was guilty. Interviewed by the *Anchorage Daily News*, one juror said, "We just didn't think they proved he did it. He may have done it, but it wasn't proved to us."

When Zieger sought to reclaim his impounded pickup truck, he was offended that troopers didn't put it back the way they found it. The seat covers, door panels, and floor mats were given back to him in a pile. The disgusted officers strongly believed that Gary Zieger had gotten away with murder, probably more than once.

Career police say that one of the great frustrations of their profession is that — for a variety of reasons — they can't always tell all they know. The painful fact is that they may not be able to prove well-grounded suspicions in court. Legal protections assure that innocent people are protected from overzealous and biased investigators. They are an essential element of the legal checks and balances in a democratic society; but they also protect some truly dangerous people.

Later, a reporter interviewed Zieger at the home of his former boss, Michael Beaver, where he was housesitting. With several friends sitting nearby, Zieger complained about his time in jail, loss of wages, his legal bill, and being behind on his truck payments.

"I don't know what I'm going to do," he said. "They jerk you off the street for five months and then they open up the door and say, 'Here you go. Have a nice day.' "

Gary went back to work at Arctic Pipelines. A.W. Beaver, owner of the company, said Arctic Pipelines had two years of training invested in Zieger, considered him a good worker and didn't want to lose him.

It wasn't the last time the detectives tangled with Gary Zieger.

In late fall of 1972, while Zieger was awaiting trial in the ZeZe Mason case, Zieger's friend, Benny Ramey, ran into Wesley Ladd, a former Cordova fisherman and cannery operator. Ladd was trying to buy Cindy's Massage Studio, a popular Spenard whorehouse. Ramey, a heroin addict, had met Ladd when the two men dug for clams near Cordova. Anchorage was girding for construction of the trans-Alaska pipeline, and hard-drinking, hard-partying pipeline workers were seen as a source of fast cash for the "entertainment" industry. Cindy's was owned in part by Ferris Rezk, twenty-eight, a hard-nosed businessman and heroin dealer who agreed to sell his interest to Wesley Ladd for ten thousand dollars. Ladd made a down payment of four thousand, and then came up with another three thousand, but was unable to find the final three thousand dollars.

Rezk was unwilling to wait for the last payment and warned Ladd that he was going to lose the seven thousand already paid unless he came up with the final payment by November 26. A day after the deadline, a snowplow operator at Angelus Memorial Park found a dead body that didn't belong in the cemetery. Ferris Rezk was found sprawled on the back seat of a 1968 Plymouth, a

.38 caliber bullet in the back of his head, his sweater pulled over his head and shoulders, and his pockets empty. A fleece-lined jacket covered the body.

Ladd, known to be buying Rezk's share of the whorehouse, was easy to find. He was interrogated, arrested, and charged with first-degree murder. Testimony in his month-long trial the following year indicated several people were present when Rezk died. Those included Wesley Ladd; Cindy Bennett, the woman for whom the massage parlor was named; Jack Anderson, Ladd's friend and a fellow fisherman; and perhaps a mysterious mob killer known only as Larry.

Ladd's lawyer was Edgar Paul Boyko, a former Alaska attorney general and one of the state's best-known defense attorneys. Boyko was a master of his trade and, by the time the case ended, observers were scratching their heads, wondering who did what to whom and why. At one point, he told the jurors that the real murderer had been in the courtroom during the trial, causing everyone to look around suspiciously.

By some accounts, Rezk was shot through a flimsy curtain as he stepped into the massage parlor's sitting room. Two witnesses said they saw Wesley Ladd with the gun in his hand when Rezk fell to the floor. Ladd himself said his gun was used in the murder but claimed "Larry" fired the shot. Other theories emerged that Ladd shot Rezk to protect Jack Anderson when Rezk became angry during a poker game. Boyko suggested that a criminal organization outside Alaska had sent the killer. He said the group was trying to take over Alaska's massage parlors in anticipation of the oil boom.

One witness testified that a man from the "Midnight Ranch" in Nevada wanted to supply women to the massage parlors in return for a share of their receipts. Among the many witnesses called by Boyko was John F. "Johnny"

Rich, a local underworld figure, gun dealer, and owner of a nude photo studio, gambling joint, and massage parlor. Rich denied that massage parlors were whorehouses but provided information about Ladd's attempt to buy Cindy's, which by then Rich owned.

At one point, a young woman described being interviewed as a prospective employee of Cindy's. "Did the interviewer explain that it was a house of ill fame?" asked prosecutor William L. Mackey.

"No," the woman answered. "She said it was a whorehouse."

When Boyko suggested that the murder was a mob hit, the prosecutor countered that if the murder took place with three witnesses, with just one bullet in the gun — and if Wes Ladd wound up with the pistol in his hand — the jury "should include in your verdict a recommendation that the organization get its money back from the hit man."

Eventually the all-woman jury deliberated for fifteen hours before deciding the stories and evidence could not be sorted out with certainty. Some believed Boyko's claims that the mob was moving in on Alaska massage parlors, though evidence was as scanty as the clothing Cindy's employees wore at work.

The jury acquitted Ladd on April 8, 1973. Boyko told reporters a special grand jury should investigate the rumored mob incursion into Alaska. A skeptical district attorney replied that the regular grand jury was meeting in frequent sessions and that Boyko was welcome to present any evidence he had. Boyko never did.

In May 1973, Trooper Colonel Dankworth ordered Sergeant Jim Vaden, a promising young investigator in the Ketchikan office, to report for assignment in the Major Crime Unit of the newly formed Criminal Investigation Bureau in Anchorage. Vaden wasn't anxious to leave Ketchikan but looked forward to working for Don Church, the unit's chief and top trooper investigator. Dankworth didn't tell Vaden that Church was about to be promoted and that Vaden soon would be moved into Church's job.

Vaden was a brilliant officer with a highly personal approach to investigations. Among other things, he believed in getting to know his quarry. When he arrived in Anchorage, Gary Zieger was the talk of the department. That summer, he called Zieger at Arctic Pipelines and asked him to meet for coffee. Zieger was surprised and nervous but curious as well. He saw it as a sign of respect, however adversarial. The two agreed to meet in a restaurant at Fireweed and C Street, a place popular with off-duty police. Zieger was suspicious and paranoid, fearing Vaden had a hidden agenda and wanted to arrest him for something. But he went.

Jim Vaden told Zieger he made it a point to get acquainted with the people he likely would arrest. He told Zieger he was an especially interesting person because he was widely feared. The two hit it off fairly well, despite Zieger's nervousness. At the end of the meeting, Zieger felt comfortable enough to ask Vaden what the detective thought would happen to him. Vaden answered that since Zieger was feared by both police and by his own friends, one or the other would do him in. He predicted Zieger would be killed in a shootout with officers or would be murdered by "friends."

While Wesley Ladd was still in jail awaiting trial, Johnny Rich picked up the expired lease on Cindy's

Massage Studio. With the lease came all the furnishings, gaudy signage, cots, mirrored ceilings, and other accouterments. By the time Ladd was set free, Rich had remodeled Cindy's and was firmly in charge of the little whorehouse in Spenard. Ladd was furious. He was still out the seven thousand dollars he paid Rezk for the lease and the prostitution trade.

On August 22, 1973, Johnny Rich disappeared on his way home from a topless bar. His sixteen-year-old pregnant wife, Bridget, and fifteen-year-old daughter, Kim, were worried. Johnny's life of crime and associates were a constant risk. His disappearance was an ominous sign. The two young women reported him missing and searched everywhere, but found no sign of him. Police conducted their own investigation. The list of people who may have been responsible for Rich's disappearance was long, but clues were few. The Anchorage underworld buzzed with rumors.

Wesley Ladd's lawyer, Duncan Webb, told investigators that Rich was out of state on a business trip and was calling occasionally to see how things were going in Anchorage. Webb said he didn't know Rich's exact whereabouts, though he was confident Rich was doing just fine. But an acquaintance told the *Anchorage Daily News* that he had known Rich for twelve years and never had known him to leave Alaska. The likelihood of a sudden trip seemed remote, too, because Rich's young wife was days away from the birth of his son, John F. Rich III.

In June, Gary Zieger had been stopped and arrested when police found stolen dynamite and a stash of marijuana in his truck. He was tried and convicted in Octo-

ber. The judge set sentencing for November 29. Knowing he was certain to be back in jail, Zieger fired his
public defender and approached Duncan Webb to rep-
resent an appeal. Webb told him that because of the
nature of the charges and evidence against him, and his
history with the legal system, a defense would be difficult and expensive. Webb wanted an advance of ten
thousand dollars. Zieger didn't have the money but decided he knew where he could get it.

Jimmy Sumpter owned two of Anchorage's most
popular topless nightclubs, the Kit Kat Club and the
Sportsman Too. He kept substantial amounts of cash in
his house and had a collection of expensive jewelry,
which he sometimes flashed in his liquor joints. Sumpter
kept late hours and often left home to visit his clubs
during the wee hours. On November 26 something woke
Sumpter about 2 A.M. He thought he heard the sound
of a window breaking in the back of his house, but decided it was not a noise but a premonition and a good
reason to check his clubs. Sumpter was at war with the
Brothers motorcycle gang, which was attempting to control the flow of topless dancers into Alaska and to orga-
nize the girls at his clubs.

As Sumpter left the house, the intruder quietly un-
locked the broken window, slipped into the house, and
went looking for cash and jewelry. When he entered the
master bedroom, Sumpter's forty-year-old wife, Marguerite, heard him and screamed. The burglar shot her
and set the bedroom afire, then ran to the basement
where he shot Marguerite's sleeping thirteen-year-old
son, Richard Merck, in his bedroom. Richard's sixteen-
year-old sister had heard her mother's screams and ran
out of the house, unseen. She returned after the intruder
left, kicking in a basement window in an attempt to rescue her brother from the growing fire. She found him
dead in his bed. Investigators said whoever killed Mar-

guerite Sumpter and her son escaped with twenty thousand dollars in cash and jewelry.

A devastated Jimmy Sumpter was determined to avenge the deaths. He offered a reward of ten thousand dollars cash. Although the reward supposedly was for information about the shootings, word on the street was that Sumpter suspected the killings were the work of the Brothers. The reward could be claimed, according to the rumor, by anyone who killed a Brother — any Brother. The Brothers, meanwhile, quickly learned that the burglar-murderer was Gary Zieger, a probationary member of the gang. The regulars considered Gary dangerously crazy and had no intention of making him a full member.

Trooper Sergeant Walter Gilmour and Anchorage City Detective Ron Rice went to Sumpter's fire-damaged house, looking for evidence and hoping to find a witness. They found one—a terrified woman across the street. She was frightened because the previous night she had seen a pickup truck with a camper shell parked outside shortly before the Sumpter house burst into flames. When the driver ran from the burning house and tried to flee the scene, the truck spun out of control and swerved into her yard. The woman had written down a license number and gave it to the detectives. The number matched to Gary Zieger's Dodge.

Detective Rice asked Anchorage Police Department dispatchers to issue a wanted bulletin for Zieger's pickup. Within hours, a patrol car found it parked behind PJ's, a Spenard strip joint. Rice drove to PJ's with Detective Stan McCartney to watch as Zieger's pickup was towed away to the police garage to be searched and its tires removed and checked against the tracks in the yard of Jimmy Sumpter's neighbor.

While the two officers waited in their car behind the strip club, Zieger showed up with his public defender.

Zieger and the lawyer opened the back doors of the police cruiser and climbed in to get out of the cold. Zieger was in a nasty mood. The last time he and Rice clashed, Zieger had made a comment to the effect of, "The next time I see you will be through the cross-hairs of a rifle."

Detective Rice says he is unsure now of Zieger's exact words, but he remembers well turning away from the wheel, putting his hand near his own pistol, and saying to Zieger, "If you put a hand in your pocket, you are a dead man."

The lawyer's mouth fell open but Zieger didn't react. The patrol car fell silent while the tow truck finished its work.

Gary Zieger was running scared. He heard about the ten-thousand-dollar reward offered by Jimmy Sumpter. Zieger was convinced that the Brothers were about to end their relationship with him to placate Sumpter. Zieger's friends said that the last time they saw him, his hands were trembling, and he was crying. He called one friend and asked for a ride. "No way," the friend replied. Zieger even asked his lawyer to call police requesting protective custody, but the request was denied.

Zieger's body was found lying on the Seward Highway at the Potter turnout. He had been killed by a shotgun blast in the chest, an unfired .357 magnum pistol stuffed down the front of his pants. The investigators interpreted the pistol as a message from Zieger's killers that he was the killer of Marguerite Sumpter and her son. Ballistics tests showed a .357 killed them but not the one found on Zieger's body. Jimmy Sumpter was in the company of others at the time of Zieger's demise.

Zieger was only twenty when he was blown away. Rumor had it that Zieger's last words to his killers were,

"Tell my mother I love her." Rumor also had it that Sumpter withdrew his bounty on any member of the Brothers, believing that Zieger's killing was sufficient showing of good faith.

Later, detectives received a tip that Benny Ramey was trying to sell jewelry, including some expensive stones that the prospective buyers recognized as belonging to Jimmy Sumpter. They found Ramey hiding out with friends in Wasilla, north of Anchorage. Ramey had with him some cash and at least one gold nugget taken from the Sumpter home. Ramey said Zieger gave him the jewels and asked him to sell them for him. Ramey was charged with receiving and concealing stolen property. The heroin addict insisted that he had nothing to do with the Sumpter killings but he began talking freely about other matters and confessed that he knew where the long-missing Johnny Rich was buried. He told a convoluted story of Rich's last days and led the investigators to an abandoned coal mine near Jonesville, seventeen miles north of Palmer.

When Benny Ramey's interview revived the Johnny Rich mystery, Jim Vaden took charge of the case, went to Jonesville, and watched as a front-end loader turned up the half-acre of mine tailings where Benny said Rich's body had been lying for months. At first, they found nothing. Then Duncan Webb's bookkeeper, Caye Mason, and her adult daughter, Virginia Pinnick, came forward saying they knew where Johnny Rich's body could be found. They led Vaden's equipment operator to the exact location. The body was buried a foot deep. With Benny Ramey and others talking, Vaden and his detectives filled in the blanks about the disappearance and murder. While awaiting trial, Ramey asked for a bail reduction. It was denied on the grounds that freedom would be dangerous to his health. Assistant District Attorney Mick Hawley told the judge that Ramey might be unavailable for a trial on account of "being extinguished."

As the story unfolded, Ramey pointed the finger of suspicion in many directions. Among other things, he said that before Johnny Rich's disappearance, Wesley Ladd had attorney Duncan Webb draw up a power of attorney putting Webb in charge of Rich's affairs and signing the massage parlor over to Ladd. Webb also wrote a "Hi Wes" letter expressing Johnny Rich's remorse for having taken advantage of Ladd's incarceration to acquire the business.

Both of the documents were to be signed by Rich, restoring to Ladd his rightful place as proprietor of Cindy's Massage Studio. To achieve that end, Ladd enlisted Ramey, who brought in his pal, the psychopath Zieger.

Ramey approached Rich at an auction house. He wanted to buy some guns. The two made arrangements to meet later at PJ's. When Rich arrived, he found Ramey and Zieger waiting for him. They asked him to go with them to Eagle River. Rich refused but Ramey and Zieger pulled out guns and forced him into the back seat of Benny's car. They drove to a cabin owned by Caye Mason, who was there with her daughter, who was Ladd's girlfriend. Ladd was there, too, having told Mason about being cheated by Rich and telling her that he was bringing Rich to her cabin because he wanted to get his property back. Then, he and Virginia could open a new massage parlor in Valdez, where the terminal for the trans-Alaska pipeline was to be built.

The plan was to force Rich to sign the documents turning his properties over to Webb, including the nude photo studio, gambling joint, and two massage parlors

— Cindy's and FiFi's. Rich protested that a power of attorney would do no good because none of the properties were in his name. Most were in the name of a girlfriend who danced under the name "Angel Dust." Ramey said Rich was stalling and whacked him on the head with a .45 caliber pistol, raising a large welt. Ladd gave Rich some ice wrapped in a towel, which Rich held against the knot on his head while he looked over the documents.

The show of humanity was brief. Johnny still refused to sign, so his captors put a clamp on his testicles and tightened it gradually, eliciting howls of pain. When he finally signed, Ladd was ready to let Rich go, but Zieger feared he and Ramey would be arrested for the kidnapping. Zieger shot Rich in the chest, but the bullet bounced off a rib without hitting a vital organ. The wounded man fell to the cabin floor and lay there, pleading for his life.

"I walked behind Zieger and pulled my own gun," Ramey said. "I was afraid of Zieger. Being emotionally disturbed as he was, he might shoot me."

Ladd then took the .45 from Ramey's hand. "Rich was lying there with his arm up, pleading," Ramey said.

Ladd pushed Rich's arm away and said, "This is for snitching on me in court." He shot Rich in the heart.

Ladd left the cabin and came back with a sleeping bag. They stuffed the body into the bag, loaded it into the trunk of Caye's car and drove to the abandoned coal mine. After they dug a hole and buried Rich, Ramey went home, changed clothes, and got a haircut. Webb asked Caye Mason to testify — if needed — that Rich signed the documents at his law office in her presence.

The next day Webb, Ladd, and Mason approached Johnny Rich's daughter, Kim, who worked at a service station. Webb told Kim her dad had left town, giving the lawyer power of attorney over his properties. He said he wanted to inventory everything immediately. Kim was stunned. Her father rarely traveled and had never left without telling her. Johnny liked to stay near the massage parlors when the money was coming in. He wanted to make sure his employees didn't steal from him.

Webb told investigators that Rich signed the documents in his presence, though the date on the papers was the day after Rich was killed. When the details of the murder scheme came out, Webb claimed he participated only because Zieger threatened him. The lawyer said Zieger bragged he already had killed three people and would "blow him away" if he didn't cooperate.

Caye Mason said she also was threatened and participated for the same reason. Virginia Pinnick testified that, after the murder, Zieger called Webb. "Hey Webb," he said. "We got it done."

The Mason family's participation in the scheme also included a charade in which Caye, Virginia and Virginia's brother faked a long-distance phone call from Caye's home intended to show that Rich was in New York after he disappeared.

As the case unraveled, Ladd called Trooper Jim Vaden from jail, where Ladd was being held on a weapons charge, and asked the detective to come see him.

Ladd said he was ready to tell all. Vaden was preparing to file murder charges against Ladd in the Johnny Rich case but decided to hear the suspect out, hoping he might get more information about the involvement of Duncan Webb. When Vaden arrived, Ladd provided more details. He tried to convince the detective that Zieger had fired the shot that killed Rich. He claimed Rich already was dead when he grabbed Ramey's .45 and pulled the trigger. Ladd said Zieger had killed the man and that his own shot was just for show to calm Zieger down. Ladd apparently didn't realize that modern pathology techniques would show definitively that his bullet was the fatal one.

In May 1975, Duncan Webb was convicted of being an accessory to a felony. He was given two years of probation and disbarred. Wesley Ladd and Benny Ramey were charged with kidnapping and murder. Ramey pled guilty and got a ten-year sentence in return for his testimony against the others. He served six years. Ladd received two life sentences, served eight years, and was released on parole.

Ramey moved to Pennsylvania after his release, fell in love, and became engaged. He sent Vaden a letter asking him to write his prospective father-in-law explaining his role in the Rich case. It is not known whether the wedding took place. However, Ramey later moved to Florida without clearing it with his parole officer. He was arrested for a parole violation and sent back to Alaska to serve the rest of his sentence.

Gary Zieger was Alaska's Billy the Kid. Like the notorious Wild West killer, Zieger was a vicious and ruthless killer who died before he reached twenty-one. The exact number of people Zieger killed is not known. One investigator estimated he was responsible for a dozen murders.

Detective Ron Rice is skeptical about speculation that Zieger killed Jimmy Sumpter's wife and stepson for money to pay a lawyer. He believes Zieger did it because he thought the murders would help him to win acceptance by the Brothers. If the rumor mill can be believed, somebody in the motorcycle gang killed Zieger himself for a similar reason.

Years after the bizarre series of crimes, Jim Vaden was asked what motivated Zieger — why the man killed so readily. Then retired, Vaden thought for a moment and said his curiosity at the time drove him to find out what made the prolific murderer tick. He thought the information might prove useful in future cases, so Vaden pursued the case even after Zieger was dead.

Zieger was attractive to women and had several girl-friends, so the detective interviewed several of them and concluded that Zieger was a conflicted, impotent homosexual or bisexual. His multiple sexual hang-ups sometimes erupted into homicidal rages. There was a more practical side to the man's aberrant personality, too. Zieger wanted to prove his casual readiness to kill, a mental mindset he hoped would prove valuable to his gangland friends. Zieger aspired to be a contract murderer. "He wanted to become the premier hired gun in Alaska, a hit man," Vaden said.

Vaden noted, too, Zieger came from a decidedly strange family. After Gary's body was found on the Seward Highway, Gary's father showed up at the Criminal Investigation Bureau office and tried to reclaim the pistol his son used to kill Jimmy Sumpter's wife and stepson. Zieger's father told Vaden he wanted it as a souvenir for Gary's younger brother.

chapter nine

A Cold-Hearted Undertaker

The new mortician's assistant was shocked to discover how the impeccable Gordon Green, a member of the Anchorage establishment, treated the dead and their grieving next of kin.

This case involves a confidential informant; funeral-home employees who reluctantly participated in the criminal activities but who cooperated with police, and bereaved families whose names never were made public. To assure their privacy, all names are fictitious except those of the defendant and investigators.

Gordon E. Green was one of Anchorage's leading undertakers. A well-dressed man with distinctive gray hair, impeccable manners, and a solicitous professional demeanor, Green offered emotional comfort to those who lost loved ones. He assured them that the mortal remains would be treated with dignity and compassion and that the family's bereavement would be eased as much as humanly possible. What nobody but his staff knew was that underneath the facade, Gordon Green had a mean streak and a larcenous heart.

Green owned funeral homes in Anchorage, Eagle River, and Palmer. His flagship mortuary was on Seventh Avenue in Anchorage; the funeral home is now long gone and the site occupied by a major oil company's Alaska headquarters. But in 1973, Gordon Green was riding high as his businesses thrived. Then, he hired a young assistant, twenty-nine-old Fred Wilson, a man with a strong sense of ethics ingrained in him at mortuary school and reinforced at his previous undertaking job in California. Young Mr. Wilson soon found that his new job offered an ethical dilemma.

Wilson's new boss often told grieving families an outrageous lie — that state law required use of a casket, even if the deceased was to be cremated. Then Gordon Green tried to sell them a casket. Green hated burning expensive caskets. Instead, after selling high-end caskets to bereaved customers who wanted their loved ones cremated, he often substituted a cheap pine box or cremated the body with no casket at all.

Then, after the family had left and the casket lid supposedly closed for the final time, Green instructed his staff to remove the body, clean up the casket, and resell it to another unsuspecting customer.

In one instance, Green embalmed the body of a young man killed in an unsolved shooting at Anchorage's Earthquake Park but kept the corpse in unrefrigerated storage. He refused for months to release it for burial until the boy's mother paid the remaining $1,500 due for his services — a serious ethical breach and a violation of state law. The woman eventually raised the $1,500 by selling her house and moving into a trailer.

Green also overcharged and sometimes double-charged clients, and he callously handled the ashes of cremated bodies — often giving the families the ashes of others while the bodies remained unburned in his back room.

When Fred Wilson arrived at Green Funeral Chapel on August 1, 1973, he was introduced to another assistant, Peter Bennett, age twenty-six, and the funeral home's manager, twenty-nine-year-old Walter Gregory. The younger assistant had been there since the previous January while Gregory, who lived above the funeral parlor, was a five-year employee. All orders came from Gordon Green.

Wilson was appalled by the lack of professionalism and a sense of decency at the mortuary. After seeing what was going on, he recruited Peter Bennett to help him protest the way clients were treated and the crimes being committed against them. The two assistants then complained loudly to Walter Gregory. They found a sympathetic ear in Gregory. By mid-September, the manager began complaining to Green, warning him that his two assistants were growing restless and dissatisfied with the way they were forced to deal with customers and the deceased. On September 19, Gregory complained to Green about the owner's overcharging for a funeral package.

Green was not happy about the criticism but did give the bereaved family a seven-hundred-dollar rebate.

The problems continued. The funeral home staff was required repeatedly to perform tasks they found offensive. Fred Wilson became increasingly uneasy. A few months later, he contacted Alaska State Troopers and offered to be a confidential informant, providing investigators with detailed information about illegal activities at Green Funeral Chapel. The case was assigned to the Criminal Investigation Bureau. For two months, investigators quietly interviewed families that had done business with the funeral home while Wilson relayed to them information from inside the mortuary.

One heart-rending case involved an infant born on Christmas Eve, 1973, which died on Christmas Day. The parents wanted the tiny girl cremated and her ashes placed in an urn for their mantel. When the father asked that the urn be engraved with the baby's name, he was told he would have to get the urn engraved himself. The grieving and confused father took the urn to a trophy shop, paid three dollars to have his child's name engraved on it, and returned to the funeral home on January 5. The parents did not want either a service or a viewing but Green's staff embalmed the child's body anyway, despite the fact that it was an unnecessary expense. The morticians told the parents that "the baby looked natural" before it was embalmed.

In fact, the baby had not been cremated by the time the father came for her ashes. Wilson told detectives that he had prepared the little body for the cremation chamber on December 28, as scheduled. But Gordon Green ordered him to terminate the operation before it began, saying he didn't want to waste the fuel for one small corpse. "Don't cremate the baby," he told the stunned assistant. "We'll stick her in with our next adult. We never cremate kids alone."

The infant's body was slipped back into the preservative tank and, when her father returned with his engraved urn, Green told Wilson to fill it with the ashes of an elderly woman from a sack lying around near the crematory. On January 9, four days after the family took home somebody else's ashes, the baby was cremated without notifying the family. Even then the indignities continued.

A twenty-one-year-old mountain climber had been killed in an avalanche in the Chugach Mountains. His father-in-law, a well-known member of an Alaska regulatory commission, selected an expensive casket and asked that the young man be cremated. After the service, following the departure of family and friends, the undertaker ordered his assistants to remove the climber from the upscale casket and put into a damaged model. "We don't cremate caskets if they are in good condition," Green told Wilson.

The substitute casket was of the type used for welfare clients. The assistants did as ordered, removing the casket's cover and placing the climber in it with the baby. Green then ordered them to put a third body into the box, that of a two-hundred-pound advertising executive. All three were incinerated together.

After the mountain climber's body was removed from the expensive casket, the mortuary assistants found that the casket's pillow had been soiled due to a gash in the back of the dead man's head, an injury sustained in the climbing accident. The funeral workers swapped the stained pillow for a clean one and stuffed the old one into the pine box with the three bodies. The upscale model then resold.

The climber's family told the funeral home that they would pick up the young man's ashes to be spread over the mountains that he loved so much. When they arrived, they were given a package containing the mixed ashes of the climber, the baby, and the advertising executive.

Meanwhile, the adman's employer, representing his family, asked the funeral home to arrange for the executive's ashes be scattered in the wilderness. Instead, what was left of the three-person funeral pyre was thrown into a dumpster behind the funeral chapel. Peter Bennett later told detectives that many clients made requests for spreading ashes over the mountains or the sea. Gordon Green promised that their wishes would be honored. Bennett had been told that a local doctor some-times handled such commemorative flights for the mor-tuary, but in the year he had been there, no such flights had been made. Instead, ashes not claimed by the fami-lies were thrown into the trash.

The burden fell to Chief Trooper Investigator Don Church to visit the infant's puzzled mother and father and ask to borrow their baby's ashes. Laboratory test-ing disclosed that the ashes in the urn contained metal from tooth fillings and pieces of adult bones. Church returned to the parents' home, telling the shocked and stricken couple what had happened.

Meanwhile, the trooper detective team was gather-ing evidence in the mortuary itself. Because autopsies frequently were conducted at funeral homes, Investiga-tor Joe Hoffbeck attended several at Green Funeral Chapel. Each time, Fred Wilson and Peter Bennett showed him what went on behind the scenes. When Wilson told him about the swapping of coffins, Hoffbeck photographed the body of the mountain climber in the expensive casket, then reached under the coffin's lining and carved his initials and the date on the inside of the box. The trooper returned the next day and took a photo of another body in the same coffin, that of an elderly man scheduled to be shipped to California.

Green also routinely steered customers away from a city cemetery where free lots were available. Instead he brought them to burial sites that charged for final resting places, a chance for Green to make yet more money by marking up the cost of the plots.

On March 21, 1974, Green was indicted by a Supe-rior Court grand jury for embezzlement and illegally holding a body for collection of a debt. The indictment shocked the Anchorage establishment, which considered the undertaker one of their own. Hours after the arrest, the family of the deceased man buried in California filed a civil suit against Green seeking damages "in excess of $10,000" for mental distress and embarrassment when they found another man's name written in his casket.

Gordon Green went to trial in May and pleaded *nolo contendere,* meaning he did not admit guilt but would not fight the charges. The mortician was found guilty of both charges and in July was sentenced to five years in prison, with all but sixty days suspended. He was ordered to stay out of the funeral business in Alaska or any other state for the length of his probation, and to pay restitution to victims in the two cases for which he was indicted.

The community greeted the sentence with mixed feelings. Spending just sixty days behind bars seemed like a slap on the wrist to many people in Anchorage especially Green's competitors and families who suspected they had been victims, too. But most were satisfied that the distinguished-looking mortician with impeccable manners who fooled so many people had been put out of business.

chapter ten

An Angry Man

---

*Muriel Pfeil walked to the parking lot
to show off her lovely new coat.
She opened the door of her Volvo,
slid behind the wheel, and died instantly
in a powerful explosion.*

Neil Mackay often joked that he learned to swim by being baptized every time he got into trouble. Mackay was born in Canada and moved with his family to California when he was two. His father died two years later and his mother remarried. His stepfather was a strict disciplinarian who enforced rules with fierce beatings. Afterward, his mother put him back on the right path by taking him to church and sprinkling holy water on him. Mackay missed his dead father terribly and his stepfather's violence made the loss seem greater. His difficult childhood affected Mackay throughout his life.

Mackay graduated from high school shortly after the Japanese raid on Pearl Harbor and invasion of Alaska's westernmost Aleutian Islands. He enlisted in

the Navy and became a Marine pilot and flight instruc-
tor in the F4 Corsair. During his service, he was injured
seriously. Military records indicated he was hurt in a
plane crash, though he told a friend it was a Jeep accident. The accident, whatever it was, resulted in back
and shoulder injuries and a steel plate in his head.

After the war, Mackay married his high school sweet-
heart and enrolled in a law school near Los Angeles. He
hated California and was sure he could make his fortune in Alaska. In 1951, with a law degree in hand, Neil
and Barbara Mackay loaded their belongings into an old
truck and headed for Anchorage. His first job in Alaska
was as vice president at First National Bank of Anchorage. He worked primarily in the mortgage department
where learned the basics of real-estate speculation. The
job gave him an insider's knowledge of what properties
were under foreclosure or soon to be foreclosed upon.

Mackay took advantage of his position and used the
inside information to buy buildings and land at bargain
prices. He also cashed out real-estate contracts, buying
property at discount prices from owners who were under financial pressure.

When he passed the Alaska bar exam in 1954,
Mackay quit the bank to open a law practice and con-
centrate on his own small but growing holdings. While
in high school in California, he had worked as an ambulance driver for a mortuary. As he described the job,
he raced to accidents, delivering survivors to the hospital and the rest to the undertaker.

Mackay drew on that experience to establish a mortuary on Fourth Avenue. He set up a law office in the
back. He soon became a millionaire.

There were two sides to Mackay. His friends saw him
as an astute businessman who could be generous when
so inclined, though even they admitted that was not often. One said he was a workaholic and became a win-

ner in both his law practice and the real estate market by working harder than his competition. Others considered him a sharp, amoral, often unethical lawyer. He seemed to worship money for its own sake, rather than what he could buy with it, and worked feverishly to build wealth.

"He was obsessed with money," said a former friend. Mackay became an alcoholic but went to Seattle for treatment and quit drinking for good.

In 1961, a committee of the Alaska Bar Association attempted to suspend his license to practice law for taking unfair advantage of a real estate client. The bar's board rejected the suspension, but the Alaska Supreme Court, then at war with the bar association, stepped in and reinstated the suspension.

"We find him unfit to continue as a member of the profession and as an officer of the courts of Alaska," the court wrote.

Three months later, the court changed its mind and reduced the disbarment to a one-year suspension. Years afterward, a new Supreme Court decided that even the suspension was excessive and cleared his record. But a bitter Mackay was convinced that the entire incident was politically motivated. His old friend and fellow lawyer, Edgar Paul Boyko, claimed that Mackay was targeted ruthlessly and brutally by the state Supreme Court.

"It's a black stain on Alaska justice," Boyko told a newspaper reporter. "I think that kind of started Mackay on a spiral down, and he's never been quite right since."

In the 1960s, Mackay did some business with members of the Pfeil family, an old Anchorage clan grown rich in real estate. Neil and Barbara lived in a penthouse apartment on top of what became the Mackay Building, a fourteen-story office tower on the edge of downtown Anchorage. It was the nearest thing the city had to a skyscraper. Muriel C. Pfeil, the matriarch of her family, bankrolled construction of a three-story annex.

In 1965, after twenty years of marriage, Barbara filed for divorce. The separation apparently was amicable. Barbara continued as his bookkeeper and property manager. However, Mackay opposed the divorce and refused to settle for three years. In 1968, the case finally went to a hearing. Mackey lost.

Barbara soon married an Iranian-born doctor practicing in Anchorage. Mackay remarried on New Year's Eve, taking as his second wife Muriel Pfeil, the 33-year-old daughter and namesake of the woman who financed the Mackay Building annex. Mackay was 45. Muriel was a hard-driving, successful travel agent.

The marriage was troubled from its earliest days. Mackay's wartime injuries kept him in pain. He suffered severe headaches and occasional seizures, and took a variety of drugs, legal and illegal. Both Neil and Muriel had strong and frequently fiery personalities. In an argument, and there were many, neither would back down. They stayed married for five years, living apart for half that time, and separated permanently two months after the birth in 1973 of a son, Neil Pfeil Mackay, who became known as Scotty.

A Supreme Court justice and friend of the Pfeil family cobbled together a settlement and wrote of their marriage and courtroom behavior: "Each of the antagonists had extremely short temper fuses and almost daily there were demonstrations of temper tantrums manifested in bitter reproaches toward each other during recesses and at other breaks, anger at the judge ... anger at opposing attorney. It seemed as a result of their temperaments that this marriage was doomed from the beginning and the only good thing that came from it was a marvelously likeable and happy child."

Their behavior went from bad to worse. Muriel claimed that Mackay abused her physically and that he blew up when she suggested that he might not be Scotty's father. He called her a pathological liar and the two got into a fistfight in the courthouse. A judge ordered both to undergo psychiatric examinations, though the results were never made public. Refusing to appear in court, Mackay barricaded himself in his apartment.

Muriel was sure that Mackay was worth $5 million and she wanted half, including real estate in which they had shared interests. When property settlement hearings began, the judge barred them from his meetings with their lawyers.

"They had tied up the court system for months," the judge explained later. "Being sympathetic to both parties, I banged heads together and we settled it. I hoped it would end the bitterness, but apparently it didn't." The judge awarded Muriel $757,000, "approximately one thousand dollars per day for the actual days they cohabited together as man and wife," plus $500 a month for Scotty's support.

Mackay was furious and balked at giving Muriel the money, though he grudgingly did. What infuriated him even more — far more — were Muriel's attempts to keep him out of Scotty's life. She tried to cut off contact between father and son. Muriel argued that Mackay was a chronic drug abuser given to violent rages and potentially dangerous to the boy. Mackay was devastated. Memories flooded back of his lost father and the constant agony of his childhood.

The judge was skeptical of Muriel's claims but Mackay's history did include drug abuse and the animosity between the two parents and her family was well known. He put a sharp limitation on Mackay's visitation rights, essentially part of one weekend each month.

Mackay wanted those rights expanded to full weekends and asked to take Scotty on a month's vacation in
Hawaii each year. Muriel was opposed both the extra
visitation and the Hawaii trips. She asked that Mackay's
suitability as a parent be reviewed and that Mackay be
denied all visitations.

On the afternoon of September 30, 1976, Muriel
Pfeil left her travel agency office to fetch a coat from
her car, parked in the employee lot across the street.
She wanted to show the new coat to her employees.
Muriel opened the door of her Volvo station wagon, slid
behind the wheel, and died instantly in a powerful explosion. Her body was torn apart by an explosive charge
placed beneath the hood, which witnesses said flew a
hundred feet into the air. The blast shattered windows
in nearby buildings and shook the ground for blocks
around. An auto mechanic ran from a nearby garage,
pulling furiously at the passenger's side door — until he
peered inside and backed away in horror.

Police detectives rushed to the parking lot and
quickly concluded that a bomb had been detonated
either remotely or with a device attached to the ignition. But they ruled out an ignition-triggered device because Muriel had driven the car ninety minutes earlier to take Scotty to a babysitter's house.
Because her car was parked in a busy and highly
visible place, it seemed unlikely the bomb had been
wired to the ignition during the interval. That suggested the explosive had been slipped under the hood
and wedged against the engine, perhaps the previous night, and detonated with a radio device held by
an assassin waiting and watching nearby. Muriel's
car keys were found on the floor of the Volvo, fur-

ther evidence that the key was not in the ignition when the bomb went off.

The investigators photographed the wreckage and marked pieces of Muriel's car found spread around the parking lot and on the adjacent street. Other detectives checked nearby office buildings and the Captain Cook Hotel, whose windows faced the lot. They scoured rooms and closets, looking for a radio-control device. Other officers combed through airline manifests to find out who had left town after the explosion.

Because of the bitter divorce and custody battle, Mackay was the immediate focus of the investigation. He was the only suspect.

Anchorage Police Chief Charles G. Anderson told a newspaper reporter that, in addition to reviewing the physical evidence, "We're also considering using a polygraph to test certain people who may be involved," a transparent reference to Muriel's pugnacious ex-husband. Fifteen detectives worked the case, including Anchorage police, Alaska State Troopers and the U.S. Bureau of Alcohol, Tobacco and Firearms, the agency with the most expertise in explosives.

Pieces of Muriel's Volvo were sent to the FBI crime laboratory in Washington, D.C., but yielded no useful evidence. After months of fruitless digging, the murder case gradually moved to a back burner, much to the frustration of detectives.

The case was unsolved, but not forgotten. Among those who vowed never to forget was Muriel's brother, Bob Pfeil, a senior pilot at Alaska Airlines. Before her death, Muriel had signed a will designating Scotty as the sole heir of her million-dollar estate with her brother as its executor. The will expressed Muriel's wish that Bob Pfeil adopt the boy.

Soon after Muriel's death, Mackay petitioned for full custody of Scotty. Pfeil was determined to keep the two

apart and to carry out his sister's wishes. He hired lawyers and fought the petition aggressively. Pfeil placed
newspaper and television ads offering twenty thousand
dollars for information on who might have arranged the
murder of his sister. No one came forward.

In December 1977, while the custody battle raged
on, Mackay got court permission for a visit with five-
year-old Scotty. Boarding a plane, father and son flew
to Hawaii, and then continued south to Micronesia. The
trip was not authorized. After a brief vacation, Mackay
left Scotty with friends on the atoll of Likiep in the
Marshall Islands, returning to Hawaii. He was arrested
in Honolulu but refused to tell anyone where his son
was hidden. Pfeil hired private detectives who found
Scotty in Likiep.

Despite Mackay's bizarre behavior, he was demon-
strably a loving father; and managed to win full custody
of Scotty in 1978. The judge overlooked what Pfeil considered to be a kidnapping and rumors about Muriel's
death. Mackay then moved with the boy to Hawaii,
where they lived in a penthouse suite in a resort hotel in
Waikiki. He told his friends he had been driven out of
Alaska by unfair and unrelenting suspicion about his
ex-wife's murder.

Pfeil was not ready to give up. He was convinced
that Mackay had arranged to have the bomb planted in
Muriel's car and he was determined to prove it. Mackay
was angered by the pilot's use of money from Scotty's
estate. The expenditures included fifty three thousand
dollars for the private detectives who found Scotty in
Micronesia, and ninety thousand in legal costs. Mackay
claimed Pfeil was stealing from Scotty.

By then, Mackay was an embittered recluse, though
he hid his anger from Scotty. Their Waikiki apartment
was littered with stacks of books and legal papers relat-
ing to the custody battle and Mackay's struggles with

Pfeil. The paperwork took up every available space, covering the desk, the dining table, and even Scotty's bed, leaving the boy to sleep where he could. Neighbors often brought food to make sure Scotty ate properly. The legal battles were unending and the animosity between Mackay and the Pfeils grew more intense.

Then on October 12, 1985, Captain Pfeil flew his Alaska Airlines jetliner back to Anchorage after a trip to Kotzebue and Nome. He landed at Anchorage International Airport, taxied to a jetway, parked, and shut down his engines. After a final check of instrument readings, he signed out his log, and headed for the employee parking lot. There, he climbed into his silver Mazda and drove toward his home at Campbell Lake.

When Pfeil was five hundred feet from home, he slowed for an intersection and a seedy-looking Lincoln Continental pulled alongside. He turned to see a young man leaning out its front window with a .45 automatic in his hand. The gunman pulled the trigger five times. One of the slugs missed and another lodged in the door. But three hit Pfeil. One caused a flesh wound, another smashed into his spine, and a third lodged in his lung. Two spent bullet casings rolled onto the pavement.

An ambulance rushed Pfeil to the emergency room at Providence Hospital, where he spoke through his pain, telling detectives he was sure the shooting was arranged by his brother-in-law, Neil Mackay. "The son-of-a-bitch finally got me," he said. The officers shared the wounded man's suspicions. Pfeil was able to give the investigators a description of the old Lincoln and a rough description of the man who leaned out and fired the pistol.

The detectives posted a heavy guard around Pfeil's hospital room. They were intent on nailing "the son-of-a-bitch" this time. Pfeil's friends were equally angry and offered fifty thousand dollars to Crimestoppers® to be used as a reward for information helping police find the two men in the Lincoln. Since the crime appeared to involve people in two states, the FBI entered the case.

Bob Pfeil's wounds were grave so he was flown to Minnesota for specialized treatment. His wife, Marianne, told reporters, "We can always hope for miracles, but I don't know. He is in good spirits, though. He's a fighter."

At the heart of the investigation were members of the Anchorage Police Department's homicide response team who first checked with their sources in the city's underworld. Several of Pfeil's neighbors reported that shortly before the shooting they noticed an old mustard-colored Lincoln at a shopping center near Pfeil's home and later parked on a nearby street. The sedan sat backward on the street, apparently so the two men inside could watch traffic approaching on Jewel Lake Road.

The team made public a description of the ambush car. Police were looking for a 1960s sedan with triple taillights and rust spots on its right side. Within days, the homicide team's commander, Detective Sergeant Mike Grimes, got word that an eighteen-year-old hoodlum named Tyoga Closson was bragging to friends that he knew something about the shooting of the Alaska Airlines pilot. Closson even told one pal that he pulled the trigger. When Grimes called on him, Closson denied knowing anything. When the detective persisted, the boy claimed he had nothing to do with the shooting but had been asked to drive the car for the shooter, whom he identified as John Bright. Closson said Bright asked him if he would like to make money doing something illegal.

"I said, 'How illegal? What are you talking about?' He says, 'Well, I need a driver cause I need to shoot somebody' I told him to get fucked," Closson told the detective.

Closson also told Detective Grimes that his friend and occasional roommate, Bob Betts, nineteen, took the job as Bright's wheelman. Closson said Betts talked to him about a pistol he owned, a nickel-plated .45 Colt automatic he said he had stolen from a lawyer's home his girlfriend was housesitting. Closson later recanted his story about stealing the pistol, claiming his girlfriend stole it and gave it to him in trade for a gram of cocaine. Closson said Betts wanted it because a .45 was more powerful than most guns available on the streets of Anchorage.

Several days before the shooting, Betts said he wanted to rent the pistol for a few days and offered to pay seventy-five dollars. Closson agreed, figuring Betts wanted to rob a Qwik Stop, and gave him the Colt. Betts said he would get the gun back to him by the next day, a Saturday. On Saturday, Betts told Closson he would need it for another day.

Asked why, Betts said, "Well, nothing happened. I'm going to need it again tonight." He said another attempt would be necessary because the first one failed. "We threw a rock through this guy's window and he didn't come out," he said.

Closson told the detective that Betts returned the pistol after the shooting and suggested Closson get rid of it. Though Betts probably meant that the gun should be thrown into Cook Inlet, Closson got rid of it by trading it to a drug dealer for a small amount of cocaine.

Detective Grimes told Closson he was in big trouble, that he could face serious charges and a long prison term because he knew about the shooting before it happened and had supplied the weapon. After much grilling, a terrified Closson agreed to talk to Betts wearing a hidden microphone and transmitter. In exchange, police and prosecutors agreed that Closson would be charged only with theft of the gun, bringing a short sentence. After serving his prison time, he would be placed in a witness-protection program.

Police rigged Closson with a wire, briefing him on questions to ask and how to behave to get the most valuable information out of Betts. It was show time.

Closson approached Betts, launched into an argument with him, and complained about his pistol being used to shoot the Alaska Airlines pilot. Betts grew angry and asked what kind of games Closson was playing.

"I told you exactly what I was going to do," Betts snarled. "You knew exactly what I was going to do with the gun."

Betts' other responses were cautious but contained enough information to convince the listening detectives that Betts had driven the car for the shooter. As their conversation ended, Closson abruptly told Betts that he had been caught and that police had offered him reduced charges. He said the officers might offer him a similar deal if he cooperated with them. When detectives called on Betts at his home afterward, they gave him the same grilling and raised the possibility of a deal. Betts eventually broke down and told the detectives that he, John Bright, twenty-one, and Larry Gentry, thirty-three, had been hired for the hit by Gilbert "Junior" Pauole, thirty-eight-year-old manager and part-owner of the Wild Cherry, a topless/bottomless club in Anchorage. Betts and Gentry were former Pauole employees. Gentry was an occasional drug trafficker and sometimes filled in for Pauole at the club on weekends. Bright, Gentry's friend and former roommate was a tough-talking street hood and former Wild Cherry bouncer whom Pauole had fired for using a baseball bat on a pimp.

Betts told the detective that Bright was the shooter. Gentry had helped them plan it and provided the car and a pistol-grip 12-gauge shotgun for a backup gun. In the end, Betts offered to roll over on the others and to draw them into conversations about the crime wearing a wire. Grimes decided to go after Gentry first.

Despite their mutual involvement, Betts and Gentry had never met. Betts went to Gentry's apartment in Midtown, introduced himself, and demanded payment of seven hundred dollars he claimed still was owed him for driving the old Lincoln the night Bob Pfeil was shot.

The encounter left Gentry confused and furious. He warned Betts not to bother him again and made vague threats.

"I'll see what I can do for you," he said, and then added angrily, "You know what I feel like doing right now. Next time you remember your fucking manners."

Junior Pauole met Seattle mobster Frank Colacurcio while serving time at McNeil Island, a federal penitentiary on an island near Tacoma, Washington. Pauole was in for possession of heroin and Colacurcio for racketeering and interstate transportation of gambling equipment. Pauole was sent to McNeil from his native Honolulu, where he was involved in a variety of illegal activities including armed robbery, drug possession, and burglary, which earned him a ten-year sentence.

Colacurcio and Pauole hit it off. After his release, Pauole became a doorman and bartender at one of Colacurcio's Seattle nightclubs. When Colacurcio was informed of trouble in one of his clubs in Waikiki, the Crazy Horse Lounge, he sent Pauole to investigate. The acting manager had told Colacurcio that Hawaii mobsters had beaten him and were demanding a thirty percent share of cash receipts. When Pauole talked to his friends in the Hawaii criminal world, he learned that the manager was lying in hopes he might land a promotion by resolving the imaginary threat himself.

Pauole's success in Hawaii prompted Colacurcio to send him to Anchorage to deal with the Brothers motorcycle gang. Colacurcio secretly owned several night-clubs in Alaska where the gang was trying to seize control of the topless dancer circuit. Pauole hired the gang's leader as a doorman and, because Colacurcio's main interest was in skimming liquor receipts, Pauole worked out a deal for the Brothers to recruit and manage dancers. The Brothers adopted Colacurcio's clubs and found they could make more money in enforcement and competition cutting, which included burning down another Anchorage nightclub, Moby Dick's.

Colacurcio was impressed with Pauole's ingenuity and appointed him manager of the Anchorage topless joints. In addition to keeping things running smoothly, Pauole skimmed up to $60,000 a month, burned the tapes from cash registers, and delivered the unreported cash to Colacurcio.

One of the clubs, the Wild Cherry, was a few blocks from the Mackay Building. Mackay also owned the building in which the nightclub was housed and was a frequent visitor when he was in Anchorage. Mackay was impressed by Pauole's mob connections.

Mackay had given up drinking but Pauole fixed him up with the club's more attractive dancers. If Mackay wanted to talk, the woman would talk to Mackay all night long. If he wanted sex, Pauole would pick up the tab and deliver the women to Mackay's apartment. Mackay was impressed by Pauole's discretion.

While trying to determine whether Pauole could arrange to have his former brother-in-law killed, Mackay mentioned that his ex-wife had been giving him trouble and that he "took care of it."

Mackay told Pauole that an old war buddy had planted the car bomb, detonating it from a half-block away. Mackay said he was having problems then with the former brother-in-law and was angry because he was sure Bob Pfeil was stealing from Scotty's estate.

Pauole and Mackay talked for two years about the possibility of arranging Pfeil's murder. Then, investigators for the Alaska Beverage Control board discovered Colacurcio's connection to the Anchorage nightclubs and revoked their liquor licenses. Pauole closed the clubs but reopened the Wild Cherry as the Fancy Moose, a no-liquor topless/bottomless club. He wanted to get back into the lucrative liquor trade and hoped Mackay might be able to get him started again in Hawaii. In early July 1985, Pauole flew to Hawaii, met with Mackay, and the two struck a deal. Later, Pauole returned, and Mackay handed him a sealed envelope containing ten thousand dollars in hundred-dollar bills. The money was to be used to hire a Hawaiian hit squad to murder Pfeil.

However, Pauole had exaggerated his Hawaiian underworld connections and couldn't deliver hit team. In fact, because Colacurcio had severed his connections with Alaska, Pauole no longer had any mob connections. So, he hired Larry Gentry, a former nightclub employee who knew a few ruthless local people. One was John Bright, whom police detectives learned was an aspiring killer for hire. Pauole knew Bright but didn't want to contact him directly, instead asking Gentry to serve as a go-between. Pauole considered Gentry to be the smarter of the two and trustworthy. Eventually Pauole asked Gentry what Bright was capable of.

"He told me he was capable of anything" Pauole said later, "and one day I just asked Larry if John Bright would do this ... He says, 'Yes, he'll do it ... he would shoot somebody.' "

When the two men accepted the assignment, Pauole gave Gentry $7,500 to be shared with Bright, with one thousand dollars to go to the driver.

Bright did his homework. He found a picture of Pfeil at the library, checked the pilot's flight schedules, followed him home, and staked out the house. He considered shooting him with a rifle from a wooded area across the street, but the pilot's flight schedule changed constantly, and his movements were unpredictable, making the timing difficult to plan.

By early October, Pauole was losing patience. Pfeil was still alive and Bright had taken to sleeping all day instead of stalking their quarry. Pauole worried that Bright intended to keep the money without doing the job. He threatened to call the whole thing off, but Gentry promised to get after Bright and put him back to work.

Days later, Bright and Betts borrowed Closson's .45 and Gentry's rusty Lincoln and lay in wait near Pfeil's home. When the pilot drove up, they pulled alongside. Bright pointed the pistol out the window and fired. After their escape, Gentry called Pauole to report the shooting. Pauole called Mackay and told him that Pfeil had been "taken care of."

Mackay responded, "Good, I was just getting ready to fight him in court," and hung up.

The next day, the news media reported that Pfeil was still alive and being treated under guard at Providence Hospital. Bright told Pauole that if he could have three hundred dollars to buy plastic explosives he would finish the job.

"I says no," Pauole later testified. "I don't want to have nothin' to do with that now. I told him, 'You're crazy.' "

Pauole asked Bright if Pfeil had seen him at the shooting. Bright said he had, so Pauole decided to get the triggerman out of town. He bought a plane ticket to Florida and gave the ticket and five thousand in cash to Gentry for Bright. In a moment of criminal brilliance, Pauole used his own name on Bright's ticket so he could get frequent-flier mileage.

Meanwhile, Detective Grimes' team was gathering information quickly and, drawing from statements of witnesses, gave the news media a description of the mustard-colored Lincoln Continental. Pauole decided to get rid of the car. He and Gentry took the Lincoln to a junkyard and gave the operator one of Mackay's hundred-dollar bills to crush it and dispose of the remaining scrap. They didn't want to arouse the man's suspicions by telling him they were in a rush, so the junkyard operator hadn't gotten around to demolishing it when police showed up a few days later.

Eight days after the shooting, Pauole called Mackay again and reluctantly admitted that Pfeil was still alive. "He's a very tough man," Pauole said. "He's hit five times."

Tyoga Closson's habit of bragging was causing the conspiracy to unravel. After Closson implicated his friends, the homicide detectives began pulling in the net. When Gentry realized that Betts had been wearing a wire during their conversations, he admitted his part in the plot and identified Bright as the shooter. He said Pauole hired the team on behalf of Mackay. In hopes of getting a reduced sentence, Gentry agreed to wear a transmitter during conversations with Bright and Pauole. Bright was cautious and uncomfortable with the discussion, but his curt comments convinced police that he had been the triggerman and that the paymaster was Junior Pauole. Shortly afterward, Betts talked to Pauole, who was cautious, too, but also managed to implicate himself.

Bright and Pauole were arrested about 10 P.M. on November 8 and held on five million dollars bail each, cash only. Both demanded to see lawyers. When Pauole's lawyer arrived, investigators showed him the evidence and played the various tape recordings. The lawyer suggested to Pauole that he help detectives gather evidence against Mackay in return for a reduced sentence. Pauole agreed. Police, the district attorney's office, and a judge offered a twenty-year sentence if Pauole would draw Mackay out and testify against him when the time came.

Worried that Mackay might receive word of Pauole's arrest, police moved quickly. At 3:00 the next morning Detective Grimes asked a judge for permission to use a wire to record conversations between Pauole and Mackay. The authorization was signed within the hour, and Pauole made the first call at 4:30 with detectives listening in eagerly. They had been after Mackay for a long time. The conversation was a classic. Mackay tried to be circumspect but his curiosity drove him to make serious mistakes. At first, he refused to take the call in his apartment for fear his line might be tapped. He gave Pauole the number for a phone in the lobby, and the two began a series of calls over the next hour. Mackay's responses were an amazing mix of paranoia and lack of caution.

Pauole indicated police were after him and told Mackay he was hiding out in Anchorage. "I'm scared," he said, "because, you know, I never do that crime. I never do that. All I did was get the money from you and give it to this guy... I don't want to go down, Mackay. If I go down, you going to go down with me because that ten thousand, you know, I never got nothing out of this whole thing."

Pauole added: "I'm a three-time loser. I'm going to go to jail for life."

When Mackay was evasive and hesitant to talk, Pauole said: "I need some help. Please help me. Don't dummy up on me."

"Well, see, here's the situation," Mackay responded, "I don't know nothing about nothing. They're trying to

lay something on you, trying to tie you in with me ...you
know it's not right, but OK, I'll see what I ... I'll do everything I can. Don't say too much, you know. You're
going to implicate yourself."

Toward the end of the third call, Mackay asked questions, apparently referring to conversations the two had
shortly after the shooting. "You mentioned something
about a metal thing. Is it ground up?"

"What?" Pauole responded. "The car? You mean the
car?"

"Yeah," Mackay answered.

Then, incredibly, Mackay asked, "What about the
G-U-N?"

"I don't know nothing about that," Junior answered.
"Those two guys got that, that uh, the G-U-N."

The ploy failed to deceive the listening detectives, who
knew how to spell gun. Two Honolulu police detectives
went to Mackay's penthouse later that day and took
him into custody. A judge ordered him held on bail of
twenty-five million dollars, cash only.

On November 11, two days after Neil Mackay's arrest, the stakes went up. While Bob Pfeil was undergoing surgery at the Mayo Clinic to remove the bullets
from his spine and lungs, a blood clot lodged in his heart
and he died. The case became a murder. Mackay, John
Bright, Larry Gentry and Bob Betts all were charged with
first-degree murder. Pauole, due to the plea agreement,
was charged with attempted murder.

At the evidence hearing on February 11, 1986 for
the other five accused—Closson, Gentry, Bright, Betts,
and Mackay—the spectator seats were filled with the
grandmothers, mothers, wives, and sisters of the younger
defendants. All were angry. Their relatives had told them

they expected to receive immunity for their assistance in the case. Betts told his family that he thought he was part of the police team. But Pauole and Closson were the only defendants who had formal agreements for reduced charges or reduced sentences.

The judge decided to try the five cases separately and, as an extra precaution, to move the Mackay and Bright trials to Fairbanks. Larry Gentry was the first to be tried, going before a jury in March 1986. When Gentry's trial began, his lawyer said the prosecution "is going to take us on a glass-bottom boat ride through the sewers of Anchorage." That promise was fulfilled many times over, with tales of drug dealing, prostitution, pimping and beatings, in addition to the murder planning and implementation.

During the trial, Junior Pauole testified that Gentry was involved in the conspiracy from the beginning and was an active and willing participant.

Gentry's lawyer argued that Pauole's word could not be trusted — that Pauole wanted to steer suspicion away from himself. The lawyer argued that Pauole was known widely as a liar, having admitted to perjuring himself in testimony before Alaska's Alcohol Beverage Control Board, a federal grand jury in Seattle, and before another jury in Portland, Oregon. Pauole also admitted to contract murder, adultery, lying to his girlfriend, cheating on his frequent-flier miles, lying to investigators for the IRS, and even lying to investigators in the Bob Pfeil murder case. Under questioning, Pauole admitted that if the Pfeil assassination had worked out, he might have taken on a few murder contracts.

Still, statements by Gentry's accomplices and other evidence convinced jurors that he had been one of the planners and had supplied the car and backup gun. Gentry, then thirty-three, was found guilty of first-degree murder and sentenced to forty years in prison with fifteen years suspended. He would be eligible for parole in fifteen years.

Two weeks later, Tyoga Closson was sentenced to eighteen months in jail for stealing the .45 used to shoot Pfeil. Judge Green told him he should "thank his lucky stars" that he wasn't charged with murder. Closson got a break because of his cooperation.

Bob Betts went to trial in August. His lawyer argued that the wheelman helped police and thought he had an immunity deal because Closson suggested the detectives might give him one. But no such deal had been made. At sentencing, Judge Green said the crime should have sent Betts away for ninety-nine years, but because he cooperated with detectives she was reducing it to fifty years. He would be required to serve at least twenty before being paroled.

John Bright was convicted of first-degree murder on October 17, a little more than a year from the day he shot Bob Pfeil, and was sentenced to ninety-nine years, the maximum. The judge stipulated that Bright, then twenty-three, would not be eligible for parole for forty years.

Mackay was a millionaire many times over and could afford the best in legal defense. He hired James Shellow, the best-known lawyer in Milwaukee. Shellow had built his reputation defending American Indian activists at the deadly 1973 siege at Wounded Knee, South Dakota.

Jury selection began in Fairbanks for Mackay's trial in January. Though all of the participants had been found guilty or had made deals, Mackay's was hardest case to prove. All other defendants were directly complicit in the plot. But the only connection between the shooter and his accomplices and Mackay was Junior Pauole. Pauole was the only one who had talked to Mackay, either face-to-face or by telephone. Despite some suspicious comments by Mackay in his phone conversation with Pauole, there was no direct evidence.

Early in the trial, the judge weakened the prosecution's case by ruling that Pauole could not testify that Mackay had told him about having his wife blown up. She also ruled out several recorded statements from Mackay's discussions with Pauole the night Pauole was arrested. She also refused to accept into evidence legal documents illustrating the court battle between Mackay and Pfeil. The documents supported the argument that Mackay had a motive to kill his ex-brother-in-law. Judge Green said conclusions about Mackay's character made in those cases could be prejudicial.

Among the tapes played for the jury was the one in which Mackay asked Pauole what he did with "the G-U-N" and whether the "metal thing" — the car — had been destroyed.

However, Mackay's lawyer argued that his client was simply playing along with what he believed was an extortion attempt by Pauole, a request for money under the threat that Pauole would try to blame Mackay for the shooting. The lawyer painted Pauole as a man on the outs with his mob bosses, desperate for cash to buy a nightclub in Hawaii and start a new life. He argued that Pauole knew Mackay would be a suspect because of the feud with Pfeil. He said Mackay had no reason to hire murderers because the thing he wanted most in life was to be close to Scotty, who was already living with him

The defense attorney called Scotty as a witness. By then a young man of fourteen, he last had seen his father when Mackay was arrested seventeen months earlier. The father and son were allowed to embrace briefly before Scotty took the stand, an emotional moment in the trial.

Mackay's trial ended abruptly after three months when the judge declared a mistrial. A two-inch stack of documents, exhibits, and other evidence was found in the jury room, some of it never authorized to be shown

the jury. Its presence could not be explained. At least seven of the jurors had read some of the material and talked about it among themselves. When a newspaper reporter interviewed the dismissed jurors, most said that the evidence against Mackay was not convincing and that they would have voted to acquit him.

Mackay was released on bail in June into the custody of an Anchorage lawyer, his first freedom since the arrest. His second trial began in November and ended on February 7, 1988 when the jury foreman declared him not guilty. The foreman later told a reporter that nobody on the panel, including two who were arguing for a verdict of guilty, believed Junior Pauole.

Following Mackay's trial, Pauole's sentence was reduced from twenty years to eighteen as reward for his cooperation in the many proceedings and for assisting federal agents looking into the activities of his old crime bosses in Seattle and Arizona. He would be eligible for parole in nine years, at age fifty.

In April, an assistant attorney general reluctantly agreed, after an appeal by Mackay to Governor Steve Cowper, that the state of Alaska should refund the five hundred one dollars Mackay paid for his return flight to Honolulu at the conclusion of the second trial. Scotty remained in Anchorage to finish high school, then went to college, and went into banking. Mackay returned to his life as a recluse. In 1994, he was found dead in his penthouse. A coroner said Mackay died of natural causes, his death unnoticed by anyone for four days.

chapter eleven

Nightmare in a Ski Town

Chris von Imhof awoke staring into the barrels of two pistols. "Are you going to shoot me?" he inquired. The masked men wanted the cash from the Alyeska Resort safe.

Frank Pierce fancied himself a criminal mastermind. He dreamed of big-money robberies and burglaries, working them out in elaborate detail while he labored at his more mundane job, laying carpet.

Frank got excited about his grandiose ideas and couldn't resist bragging about them to friends. He was thirty-three, a drug-user, a biker, and a member of "The Family," Anchorage's leading gang of toughs. Members of The Family often did strong-arm work for organized crime, which had been attracted to Alaska by the flow of money during construction of the trans-Alaska pipeline.

As winter faded in 1978, Pierce and a partner were hired to replace worn carpet in the ski lodge and two-story office building at Alyeska Resort in Girdwood, a small recreational community forty miles south of Anchorage. The resort management asked the carpet layers to finish their work as quickly as possible. Spring was the prime skiing season, when days grew longer and temperatures warmed. Skiers would be coming to Alyeska by the thousands.

Pierce knew that many skiers had money to spend, and spent it heavily on their sport, paying with cash and checks for lift tickets, equipment rentals and, especially for entertaining each other in the resort's bars and restaurants. The season peak would be the three-day weekend of Spring Carnival in early April. The skiing would end when the lifts closed on Sunday, but the partying would continue until the bars closed late that night. The resort did not use an armored car service, so its office safe would be jammed with three days of receipts awaiting the opening of banks in Anchorage on Monday morning.

Pierce used his access to the hotel, the day lodge, and the nearby office to plan his grandest scheme ever. He learned about the resort operations chatting with resort employees. Once, in late March, stopping in at the gift shop, he ask questions about Chris von Imhof, the resort's general manager — questions that employees would remember weeks later.

Spring weekend was a huge success, the best in the thriving resort's history. An estimated five thousand people had visited the resort on Sunday. By that night, Chris von Imhof was exhausted. He had a fine team of employees who kept things running smoothly, but as general manager, he was called to resolve the more nettlesome problems and be available morning, noon, and night. Von Imhof's office was a short drive from his home in Girdwood. His wife, Nina, and her brother, Lon Whaley, had stayed up to watch the late movie and it was after midnight when Chris wearily climbed the stairs to his bedroom. His six-year-old son, Chris Jr., had fallen asleep in the bed. Chris was too tired to move him, so he climbed in beside the boy and quickly drifted off. The Von Imhof's nine-year-old son, Rudi, was asleep in another room.

Downstairs, Lon and Nina heard a dog barking outside, but seeing nothing out the window, they went back to their movie. In the Von Imhof household, the last one to bed customarily locked the doors and put out the lights. That never happened on Sunday night.

A few minutes later, two men in ski masks and dark clothing slipped quietly into the house through the front door. They could see a light flickering from the TV room. They burst in into the room, pointed pistols at Lon and Nina, and ordered them to raise their hands. Whaley stood up but put his hands in his pockets, assuming the masked men were friends playing a joke. When one pulled back the hammer on his pistol, Whaley threw his hands in the air. This was no joke.

At first Nina was hysterical but she quieted quickly when one of the robbers hit her in the face.

"Who else is in the house?" the man demanded.

Whaley told him Chris von Imhof and the boys were upstairs. "What do you want?" he asked. "What are you after?"

"Don't worry," the second man replied. "We're just after the receipts."

The men pushed Whaley to the floor and Nina von Imhof onto a couch. They forced both to lie on their stomachs, tied their hands and feet with wire, and then covered them with blankets.

Upstairs, Chris von Imhof awoke staring into the barrels of two pistols. "Are you going to shoot me?" he asked.

The men said they were after the money in the resort safe. They tied Von Imhof hand and foot with wire, too, while demanding his office keys, the combination to the safe, and instructions how to deactivate the alarm system.

Von Imhof told the robbers that he couldn't remember the safe combination because he rarely dealt with cash or the bank deposits, but he said he could tell them where to find his keys and offered to tell them about the alarm system. Yet, the robbers thought the resort manager was stalling, and grew angry and threatening. The sounds of their shouting alarmed Nina von Imhof and Whaley downstairs.

One of the men asked who would be at the office at that time of night. Chris von Imhof said the only possibility was a night auditor at the hotel's front desk. The man who seemed to be in charge left the house while his partner stayed behind to guard the hostages.

As he lay hog-tied, Von Imhof tried to remember where he had heard that voice before.

Paul Aubert was deep into paperwork when he heard a noise behind him and glimpsed a man in a ski mask and black coat coming through the hotel office door with a pistol drawn. The intruder grabbed Aubert's head and twisted it away, preventing him from getting a close look. The man took off Aubert's glasses, effectively blinding him, and then found a key to nearby Room 108, where he tied Aubert to a bed with wire and gagged him with strips of bed sheet.

The robber seemed solicitous, telling Aubert he would not be hurt, and taking care not to let the wire cut off circulation in the auditor's hands or feet. The robber said he would be in the office next door for about an hour. He asked how sensitive the alarm system was. Aubert said it sometimes went off when a squirrel walked across the windowsill. The robber left the hotel room but later returned, removing the gag and demanding the key to the cash drawer at the front desk. Aubert did as ordered but asked the intruder not to tie the gag so tightly, saying he was having difficulty breathing. The robber loosened the gag, and then left again. Aubert worked his hands loose several times, but each time the robber returned and bound him again.

The ordeal continued for more than four hours. The first robber returned to the Von Imhof home several times and demanded more information from the resort manager, each time getting nothing useful and driving off angry. He couldn't get the safe open and the night auditor didn't know the combination either.

Several times, the Von Imhof's phone rang once, fell silent, and then rang again — some sort of signal. The robber guarding the hostages would answer and talk quietly into the phone. At one point, the phone rang the same way while both robbers were in the house. The two men had an accomplice.

The robbery was not going according to plan. The gunmen became increasingly nervous and frustrated. Whaley grew worried that they were becoming dangerous. He tried humor to calm the man guarding the house. Once, when the phone rang, he shouted from beneath his blanket, "I could get it but I'm all tied up right now."

State Trooper Bill Hughes, the only trooper posted at Girdwood, had been busy during the Spring Carnival too. Exhausted from a series of fourteen-hour days dealing with the large crowds and unruly revelers, Hughes crawled into bed Sunday evening after a quick dinner. Just after 10:00, his phone rang. It was John Trautner, owner of Girdwood Texaco at the intersection of Seward Highway and the Alyeska Highway, the main road leading into Girdwood and the Alyeska Resort. Trautner said a driver had blasted through a stop sign at the end of the resort highway, skidding across the main highway, and dropping down an embankment. The car plunged one hundred thirty feet into the marsh and the driver took off running. Trautner was about to tow the car out of the mud when he noticed it contained numerous Michelob beer bottles, many of them empty.

Hughes, a young man with just two years on the force, threw on his clothes and drove the short distance to the accident scene. A ten-year-old Chevrolet sedan was embedded in the mud. Hughes soon found the driver walking north toward Anchorage on the Seward Highway. Hughes ran two field tests — walking a line and reciting the alphabet backwards. The man was drunk. The trooper arrested him for drunken driving, helped him into the rear of his patrol car, and drove to the detachment headquarters in Anchorage. When the driver failed a Breathalyzer test there, Hughes filled out arrest forms and drove him to the lockup. The weary officer headed home and crawled back into bed at 3:30 A.M.

The hostages kept working at their bonds, trying to get free. Eventually Nina von Imhof got her hands loose.

"What do I do?" she asked her brother. He cautioned her to stay put for fear the robbers might take the children hostages. She put her hands behind her back and pretended to be tied.

At the resort, the night auditor also freed himself, left the hotel room, and crept back to the front office. He retrieved his glasses and phoned for help while hiding behind the door. Meanwhile, the robber returned to Room 108, found the auditor missing, and took off in a hurry toward the parking lot. The gunman was gone, much to Aubert's relief.

Trooper Hughes had been in bed about forty-five minutes when his phone jangled once again. His dispatcher in Anchorage told him an armed robbery was in progress at the ski resort. "Are you awake enough to understand what I'm telling you?" she asked.

The question was unnecessary. Adrenaline had taken over and Hughes was pulling on his clothes, his mind racing.

"Backup cars are on the way," she added as he hung up the phone and ran for his cruiser.

Hughes lived on Cortina Road, a few blocks from the hotel. He sped through the resort's ice-covered parking lot, came to a skidding stop, and jumped out. Running the last few steps to the office building, he approached with his gun drawn. The office was quiet, but the entrance door hung loose on its hinges and had a large sneaker footprint in its center. Somebody with a big foot had kicked it in.

Whoever had been there was gone, but the robbers had left a mess. Empty money trays and papers were scattered around the office. Debris covered the floor. The safe sat in the middle of the room, open and empty, the mess suggesting that somebody had blown it open — or tried to. A closer look showed the massive safe door had been peeled open with a heavy-duty crowbar and a punch, a criminal technique requiring equipment, leverage, and considerable strength. Much of the debris was dust and insulation from the destroyed door.

At the Von Imhof home, the man guarding the family left briefly, then came back and told them the night auditor had escaped. "Looks like the jig is up," he added. "I've got to find my own way home. Give me fifteen minutes. I've been nice to you guys."

As the robber left the house for the final time, Nina untied her brother and then ran upstairs to untie Chris. Lon Whaley grabbed a .30-06 rifle and went prowling through the nearby streets of Girdwood, looking for the men who had terrorized the family. Chris von Imhof grabbed his own rifle and headed for the office.

Trooper Hughes hurried out of the shambles of the resort office and headed across the narrow walkway to the hotel, where the night auditor still hid in the front-desk suite. Movement in the large parking lot caught the officer's eye. He turned to see what looked like a vehicle sneaking away with its lights off. The driver slowed at the lot entrance and his brake lights flashed, giving him away. The robber floored his accelerator and sped off down Alyeska Highway.

Hughes scrambled back across the lot to his patrol car and headed for the highway. As he left the lot, he could see a van rounding a curve at the bottom of the hill. But when the trooper reached the curve, the van was nowhere to be seen. Near the Seward Highway intersection, he overtook a pickup truck ambling down the road; its windows frosted over. He had seen the suspect vehicle only briefly, but knew it was not a pickup truck. Hughes pulled the pickup over to ask if the driver had seen a passenger van come speeding by. Before stepping from the patrol car, he routinely called in the pickup's license number.

The driver was a woman. A man sat in the passenger's seat. Both were shivering and appeared underdressed for the weather. The two said they were on their way to work but had gotten a late start and hadn't had time to warm up the truck. Hughes knew most Girdwood residents and didn't recognize this pair, but many unfamiliar faces were in the village that weekend. When the couple said they had not seen any other drivers, he sent them on their way and resumed his search for the vehicle he had seen fleeing the resort.

Hughes cruised the side roads of Girdwood, but found nothing.

Meanwhile, troopers were setting up roadblocks north and south of Girdwood on the Seward Highway, and one on Alyeska Highway itself, the only road out of the resort. Hughes drove the main highway toward Anchorage until he met a southbound patrol car near the roadside community of Indian, and then returned to Girdwood and the Von Imhof home. There he listened, taking notes, while two Criminal Information Bureau officers interviewed Whaley and the Von Imhofs. The hostages said their assailants wore dark coats and jeans; one of them wearing boots and the other sneakers.

During the interviews, a detective asked Lon Whaley if he noticed anything unusual about one of the pistols carried by the robbers. "No, but it was pointed at me, and that was unusual," Whaley replied.

Trooper Hughes missed part of the conversation and didn't realize that the hostages were talking about two different men. Their descriptions were so similar that they could have talking about a single suspect. Several neighbors volunteered that they had seen two men wearing strange-looking wigs near the Von Imhof place the night before the robbery.

Then, troopers got a break. About 8 A.M., a motorist stopped at one of the roadblocks and reported seeing a hitchhiker south of Bird Creek who was acting strangely. The man was standing beside the road with his thumb out, but when a car approached he ran to the side of the road and hid. She saw the man only briefly, but he appeared to come back out onto the road after the car passed and begin hitchhiking again. Hughes headed north on the highway again until he met another patrol car coming south. Neither officer had seen anything.

A trooper helicopter swept down over the mudflats beside the highway. The suspect, seeing the northbound cruisers pass, thought he was in the clear and returned to the highway where Hughes found him as he drove over a small rise near Bird Creek. Hughes approached cautiously while the helicopter hovered nearby. The man fit the description that Hughes heard given by the hostages and even wore a ski mask rolled up on his head.

The copter pilot radioed Hughes that he had flown over the man at low level, and the suspect never once looked up. That seemed like strange behavior.

"Take your hands out of your pockets slowly," demanded the young trooper, his weapon drawn, "and hold your hands out where I can see them."

The trooper patted the man down and found a .38 snub-nose revolver in one of his coat pockets. His identification showed he was Frank R. Pierce, Jr.

Pierce claimed he had found the revolver and that his backpack contained only dirty clothes. Hughes opened the pistol and found it loaded with hollow-point bullets, a nasty cartridge that expands on impact and creates a massive wound. Hughes confiscated the pistol, ordered the man into his car and advised him of his rights. He waved thanks to the helicopter just before it turned away.

"Where were you headed?" the trooper asked.

"Seward," Pierce answered.

Asked where he was coming from, Pierce said, "Anchorage"

"Then why were you walking northbound?" Seward was in the opposite direction.

"I wasn't," he said.

"Would you mind coming with me to Alyeska?" Hughes asked. "I'd like to have you talk to an investigator there."

Pierce didn't seem anxious to meet anyone.

"I'll tell you what," Hughes said, "if it turns out you didn't have anything to do with this robbery, I'll drive you halfway to Seward and you can hitchhike from there." The suspect agreed.

Before they pulled away, Pierce showed Hughes where he had found the gun, just north of the place the trooper picked him up.

Sam Barnard and another detective met Hughes and his suspect at the resort. The officers had been interviewing the night auditor, who showed them red ligature marks on his neck and wrists. Hughes explained to the detectives why he stopped Pierce and told them about finding the .38 in the man's pocket.

Barnard asked Pierce if he could look into his backpack. Pierce answered, "No."

"If you don't give us permission," Hughes said, "we'll have to try to get a search warrant."

Pierce grimaced, realizing the cause was lost, and agreed. Inside the pack, troopers found clothes and envelopes stuffed with $60,000 in cash, checks, and credit-card charge slips. Pierce claimed he had found the money near where he found the .38, just before Trooper Hughes arrived.

"Well," Pierce said, "I thought I struck it rich, you know?"

"Have you ever been in this office right here before?" Barnard asked.

"I laid the carpet," he answered.

Barnard's written report of the robbery that day noted that whoever broke open the safe almost certainly would have residue from the safe's torn insulation on his clothing.

Pierce was taken to the Anchorage jail and booked for burglary not in a dwelling, a simple charge based on his possession of the money. That would hold him until further investigation would justify charges based on the robbery. His clothes were confiscated and he was given jail garb.

The media quickly jumped on the story about the bizarre robbery and the arrest. When Pierce's friends heard the news; none were surprised, most decided to keep quiet.

Frank's twenty-three-year-old sister, Grace, visited him in jail the next afternoon. A few hours later, she and her roommate, Tracy Hupp, drove to a side street in the highway neighborhood of Indian and retrieved Frank's van from where it had been left after his high-speed run from Girdwood. Police were searching for the van but had not yet checked the small, unpaved road where he left it. Grace used a hideaway key that Frank kept in a magnetic box under the car and drove it back to Anchorage while Tracy drove the pickup.

The next day, an Anchorage patrol car spotted the van parked outside Grace and Tracy's apartment. Investigators made a call on the women, asking if they had removed anything from the van. Grace said she had taken a bag of clothes from the back and washed them. She said she thought Frank might need clean clothes in jail.

The detectives confiscated the van and the clothes, and brought in a mechanic to dismantle the building's washing machine and to remove debris found inside. They also removed residue from the back of the van and found a wig that resembled the one described by the Von Imhof's neighbors. The evidence was sent for analysis to the FBI laboratory in Washington, D.C.

Back in Girdwood, Hughes talked to several people who had seen two men hanging around in the hotel bar late on the night of the robbery, apparently waiting for other customers to clear out.

The detectives had a strong case against Pierce but did not know the identity of the robber at the Von Imhof home. They suspected Grace Pierce had been a lookout. The license number of the pickup truck stopped by Hughes on the morning of the robbery was registered to Grace, but Hughes had not looked closely at the driver or passenger when he stopped them on the morning of the robbery. He had been anxious to pursue the van and had not asked for identifications either. Grace claimed she had loaned the truck that day to a woman she didn't know who wanted to use it to look for a job. No charges were filed against her.

The investigators also looked at the unsavory cast of characters with whom Frank Pierce had lived, worked, and associated. They had their favorite suspects, including William R. "Beef Stew" Stewart, a sometimes roommate who worked sporadically at a motorcycle shop. Police interest in Stewart grew intense on May 11 when they received a call from Florida from Ron Robinson, a twenty-three-year-old who owned a home in Anchorage and had been renting it to Stewart, a man he knew as "Mad Dog" and an Alaska Native woman known only as Gloria.

Robinson said that before he left for Florida, Stewart had confided to him that he was involved in the Alyeska robbery, and that both Stewart and Frank Pierce had money stashed away. Robinson told them that Stewart was Grace Pierce's boyfriend. He said he was afraid of Stew, which he said was why he had not reported the information earlier.

Detectives visited Robinson's house and interviewed the three people living there. Mad Dog, whose real name was Robert R. New, said Robinson had asked them to look after the house until he could sell it.

Pierce was bailed out on May 12. He went immediately to state trooper headquarters to retrieve his van and confiscated clothes — a sweater, shirt, pants, jacket, shoes, and socks. He was told that he could have the van but his clothes were being held as evidence. Pierce, outraged, argued that the clothes were all he had to wear and troopers had no right to keep them from him.

A few weeks later, the reason for Pierce's concern became obvious. On June 6, the FBI Lab reported back on its analysis of Frank's clothing, confirming that the debris from both the clothes and the washing machine appeared to be insulation from a safe, possibly the one ripped open in the Alyeska Resort office.

On June 23, Pierce and Stewart were indicted on charges of burglary in a dwelling, burglary not in a dwelling, and armed robbery. Stewart was arrested later that day. The arresting officer said that en route to jail,

Stewart said he might be willing to talk about the robbery if he could get a deal. When the officer advised
prosecutors of Stewart's offer; they replied that no such
deal was likely. Stewart stopped talking.

In late July, Nina von Imhof heard from a friend
who lived in Indian that two of her friend's neighbors
at Bird Creek were talking about Frank Pierce. Their
house was next to the Bird Creek Sawmill, about one
hundred yards from where Frank abandoned his van.

The neighbors, two men, told Nina's friend that
Pierce had invited them to take part in the Alyeska robbery. They declined. When detectives interviewed the
pair, they learned that Pierce liked to plan robberies in
his head, then to brag about his ideas to friends. The
men had not taken him seriously at the time.

The .38 that Pierce carried was traced to an Anchorage hardware store. It was one of three guns
bought by David Earley, age twenty-two. The store clerk
said Earley was a nervous customer who came into
and left the store through the back door. He bought
the three pistols, dropped them into a paper bag, and
left without the cartons or paperwork that came with
the guns. Though the customer's behavior was bizarre,
the clerk said he had no reason not to sell the pistols to
Early, who climbed into a car with another man about
the same age.

"The world is full of strange people," the clerk
thought. If he sold guns only to "normal" people, he
would never make a sale in this town.

Detectives tracked down and interviewed Earley.
He told them the pistols were stolen from him at gun-
point shortly after he bought them. He said he was
laying on the floor of a van, strung out on acid, when
robbers opened the van door, flipped him over onto
his stomach, and left with the sack of weapons and all
his money — several thousand dollars. Asked if he knew

Frank Pierce, he said he had been introduced to him by an acquaintance named Tim Knickerbocker, to whom he had shown the guns just before they were stolen.

Chris and Nina von Imhof and Lon Whaley were shown Stewart in a police lineup. They listened to man reading words their captors had used. Chris made a positive identification. Nina and Lon said they recognized Stewart but were somewhat hesitant, making the identifications inconclusive.

The only real evidence against Stewart was the claim by Robinson that Stewart told him about participating in the robbery with Pierce. But Robinson wanted restitution for damage to his vandalized apartment, so his motives for making the statement were suspect. Prosecutors decided the case would not hold up and decided not to bring it to trial. The charges against Stewart were dropped.

Though the detective team strongly suspected that Grace Pierce was the lookout, those suspicions could not be proven either. Hughes looked at a photo lineup that included Grace's photo, but could not pick her out. In desperation, prosecutors had Hughes hypnotized in hopes that he would recall the face of the woman driving the pickup.

Unfortunately, the lineup and hypnotism took place seven months after the robbery. Hughes had stopped too many drivers by then. Recalling the face he had seen so briefly was impossible.

The detectives even called on John Trautner, the Texaco station owner who also saw the pickup driver. He tried without success to pick her out from a photo lineup, leaving the investigators with nothing to use against Pierce's sister either. No charges were filed.

The following March, Pierce was convicted by a Superior Court jury of armed robbery, burglary in a dwelling, burglary not in a dwelling, receiving and concealing stolen goods, and carrying a concealed weapon. He was sentenced to multiple eleven-year terms in prison, to be served concurrently.

chapter twelve

A Young Girl is Missing

The abduction of the little girl with long blond hair struck fear into the heart and soul of the close-knit highway community. Had she been taken by one of their own?

Mandy Lemaire, eleven, lived in a log home in the rural village of Tazlina, population 241, about thirty miles west of Glennallen. Despite her age, she had spent more time hunting and fishing with her dad than most kids do with their fathers in a lifetime. The great Alaska outdoors was just beyond her doorstep. Bears and moose lived in the surrounding forests, but young Mandy knew how to behave around wild creatures, how to maintain a respectful distance, and how to avoid confrontations.

The first day of the 1991 school year was nearing and Mandy was about to enter the sixth grade. Her friend Erin lived three-quarters of a mile down the road and the two girls wanted to get together that

Thursday, August 22 to play. Their homes were near the busy Richardson Highway, but set off from the traffic on a two-lane rural road known as the Tazlina Terrace Drive.

Mandy kept bugging her mother, Valerie, about going over to Erin's house. Then Erin called just before 3:00 to ask if she could come to the Lemaire house instead. Valerie Lemaire agreed and watched as her daughter left the house, her long blond hair flowing over a pink jacket. The two friends agreed to meet midway between their homes and then return to the Lemaire house. Mandy's bike had a flat tire, so she set off walking along a neighborhood airstrip near the road. Valerie Lemaire worried about her daughter walking by herself, but neither of the girls would be alone for long.

A half-hour later, Erin showed up at the Lemaire door alone. She had walked all the way and seen no sign of Mandy. Valerie assumed that the two kids somehow had missed one another, but she was worried. Mandy was a dependable girl. If she said she would meet Erin, she definitely would do so.

Valerie alerted her husband, Dave, and the two parents hurried off with Erin, calling to Mandy, hoping she might have ducked off the road to avoid an animal and become lost momentarily.

Finding no sign of their daughter, they alerted friends and neighbors and soon a community-wide search began, drawing in about one hundred volunteers. Within two hours, Dave was in the air with a pilot friend, flying a search pattern over the area. Ground parties combed the forest floor as new ones organized. It seemed unlikely that Mandy would be lost for long. The area was laced with trails used by all-terrain vehicles, all leading back to the highway.

Mandy's dad, a long-distance trucker, believed that Mandy's backwoods know-how made it unlikely that she was lost. "You could have blindfolded her or anyone else and dropped them in one of those areas and turned them loose and they would have made it home," he told a newspaper reporter. "She knows those roads."

The missing-child report triggered a rapid response from Alaska State Troopers at Glennallen. Troopers launched their own search, using helicopters to fly at low speed and a tracking dog to follow Mandy's trail leading from her home. The dog picked up Mandy's scent, following it to a point midway to Erin's house, and then lost it. A neighbor told troopers he had seen Mandy near that spot shortly before she disappeared.

Dave Lemaire now feared the worst — a human predator had taken his daughter. "The highest probability is she was picked up by somebody," he said. "That thought flashed through my mind during the first fifteen minutes we were looking for her."

Police wondered if Mandy might have run away. Two thousand children run away every year in Alaska — some for a few hours, some forever. But Mandy was unlikely to be a runaway. She and her family were close. Mandy had earned her parents' trust. She always kept her word.

"She's a very responsible and very mature little girl for her age," Valerie Lemaire told an Associated Press reporter.

Both parents were proud to say theirs were not latchkey children. Mandy and her siblings were thoughtful, cautious, and well schooled in the dangers of the world.

Late Friday, Mandy's nine-year-old brother, Daniel, went to search headquarters at the local fire station. He watched glumly, a sunken look on his face, as search teams checked off areas that had been covered.

"There are only two more left," the boy moaned.

On Saturday, troopers searched vehicles and roads within one hundred miles of Glennallen while volunteers drove up and down the Richardson Highway, walked and rode all-terrain vehicles on remote roads and trails off the highway, searched the dense underbrush, and checked abandoned buildings. Troopers ruled out an attack by a wild animal. If an animal had attacked Mandy, signs of the attack would have been found.

Others came to the firehouse with food, drinks, and baked goods for the volunteers. Late Sunday night, the troopers called off their forest search and announced that the disappearance was a probable kidnapping, a determination that brought the FBI into the case. Volunteers continued to scour the ground throughout the area. Others gathered at the general store and used its copying machine to make fliers that could be carried statewide by Dave Lemaire's fellow truckers.

"It's like she just evaporated," said Trooper Sergeant Bud Dial. "We're treating it as an abduction or kidnapping."

Mandy's parents waited next to the phone. Dave Lemaire decorated his daughter's room with purple balloons and ribbons, in the faint hope he and his family later would welcome her home. He said he was trying to drive away thoughts that something terrible might have happened.

"I'm numb," he said. "I'm frustrated. The thing to do is keep a cool head. All that we can do at this point is wait for the phone to ring."

When his strength waned and awful thoughts took over his mind, he came to feel it might be better to find his daughter's body than to think she had been in the hands of a kidnapper so long.

Valerie Lemaire reluctantly stayed at home with her two sons. "It's got to the point where I don't want to stay home," she said. "I want to go out and do something. If something happened to her, I will deal with that when the time comes. But right now, you just have to have a lot of hope that something will happen and they will find her."

On Wednesday, nearly a week after Mandy's disappearance, Sergeant Dial revealed that troopers had a lead. He declined to give any details, but said: "We've got some information that is encouraging. We're hoping it works out."

From the start, some Tazlina residents speculated among themselves that Mandy might have been taken by one of their own, perhaps even someone participating in the search. The girl knew not to accept a ride from a stranger, but she might have climbed in with somebody she knew, especially if she thought the person would be offended if she refused. People tried to remember if anyone had been acting weird.

Weird is a relative thing in Alaska's rural areas. Small and remote communities attract a mixed bag of people. Some are simply repulsed by urban life and drawn to the edge of wilderness for its serene beauty. Some are running from something — often themselves. Still others are known as end-of-the-roaders who simply want to get as far from civilization as possible without actually leaving it. Small communities near the end of the road system attract those who want to live on the edge, where privacy is respected.

Experienced police officers know what to expect from their communities. Coming into a rural area and asking people to identify neighbors they considered strange would accomplish nothing. Most wouldn't know where to start. But even in such woolly and diverse company, potential suspects have a way of drawing attention to themselves.

Troopers told the community that further searching seemed hopeless. There was no place left to look. But local people refused to give up even though it was hunting season and time to lay in a winter's supply of game. Cherie Ansell, an emergency medical technician in Copper Center, organized volunteers to do a thorough reworking of a three-square-mile grid around the spot where the police dog lost Mandy's trail.

"We didn't feel comfortable about how the ground had been covered," she said, "so we came back and literally searched it hand to hand. We wanted to be a hundred percent sure instead of ninety or ninety-five percent sure. It doesn't sound like a lot of ground until you start walking every foot of it. Some of it is very rough terrain."

The terrain was densely wooded and bordered by the natural bends of the Copper River and the unnaturally straight line of the Richardson Highway. Civil Air Patrol planes flew patterns overhead while ground crews combed the brush around roadside pullouts, beat through the forest, pushed aside overhanging bushes, and peered into culverts, abandoned cars, and vacant homes.

A volunteer found the body of Mandy Lemaire in a ditch a mile from her home. It had been ten days since she disappeared. She lay in an uninhabited wooded area penetrated by a few rough roads. It was an uncompleted subdivision containing only falling-in cabins and rusted cars — a place that had been searched.

Dave Lemaire was trudging through woods in nearby Chitina when a fellow searcher approached and quietly told him the news. Dave drove disconsolately home to his stricken wife and their two sons. Later that day, an *Anchorage Daily News* reporter found him walking down the airstrip behind his house, retracing Mandy's last steps. Asked how he was holding up, he said, "I was angry and relieved; whatever monster did this not only tormented a little girl but also her father, mother and family, and this community."

The investigators spread yellow crime-scene tape around the entire section of woods and sent the body to a medical examiner. They knew from their own inspection that she had been shot twice in the head with a small-caliber weapon and had been raped. For fear the information would help the killer and serve only to traumatize the family, they would say only that she appeared to have been murdered. They declined to say how or when they thought she was killed and asked the searchers who found her not to give out any information.

The day after Mandy was found, balloons still hung on Mandy's bedroom door. Dave Lemaire grilled red salmon for the grieving family and friends. It was his daughter's favorite meal and cooking helped him take his mind off the horrifying news. But the agonized father said he found comfort only in knowing that Mandy's ordeal, whatever it had been, was over.

Lieutenant John Glass, commander of the trooper detachment in Palmer, said the investigators were looking at several people of interest. "We have not honed in on any one person," he said. "We do have several people that we're looking at."

The discovery hit the community hard. If the murderer was a local man, he might still be among them. The location of the body added to speculation that the killer was one of the searchers. If so, he would know what areas had been combed and could have moved Mandy's body after the spot was checked off at search headquarters.

Parents were afraid to allow their kids walk the roads alone, even for school. Many drove or walked them to their classes or to the bus stop, then met them after school. A counseling team came in from Anchorage and held a community session at the school gymnasium.

"A lot of people moved here to get away from this kind of thing," said one woman, a thirty-year resident of Glennallen. A man added: "This is a close-knit community, even if we're spread out over a couple hundred miles. You just feel like it was one of your own."

By then, eight investigators from Anchorage, Fairbanks, and Palmer were working on the case, tracking down tips from the public and examining scraps of evidence from where Mandy's body was found. The team met every morning at 8:15 to discuss the newest leads and to divide up the information for follow up. Then, they worked on the case through the day and often well into the night. A Crimestoppers® spot ran on the local television station asking for the public's help. Sergeant Dial said the intent was to jog the memory of anyone who might have seen something suspicious.

"We've had some very encouraging leads," he told the news media, but as before, he added only: "I can't tell you about them."

Among clues withheld was the report of the medical examiner — Mandy had been shot twice in the head with a .22 and raped with an inanimate object.

As time went by with no arrest, frustration and anger grew. One Glennallen man said, "I'd like to see a vigilante outfit hang the son of a bitch from a tree."

The community joined Mandy's family for a memorial service at Grace Baptist Church. The ceremony attracted some two hundred fifty people, more than the entire population of Tazlina. Some in the audience wept when a group of young girls sang "Friends Forever."

The death of the little girl touched hearts throughout Alaska and many people asked what they could do to help. The family suggested that contributions be made to Dollars for Dogs so the organization could buy and train for the Alaska State Troopers a new dog — a K-9 officer like the one that followed Mandy's trail to the place where she had been abducted. Contributions flooded in.

One of the main worries of investigators was that the murderer might kill again before they could find him. It also occurred to them that he might have accosted a child in the area before. Securing permission from the Copper River School District, troopers contacted the Standing Together Against Rape organization, which sent volunteers to speak to the district's six hundred students. STAR told youngsters how to protect themselves from physical and sexual assault. The children were asked if any adults had approached them inappropriately or assaulted them. Parents were barred from the presentations so the children would feel freer to speak out, but some parents were furious, suspecting that questions about past assaults might be looking for more than just potential rapists and murderers.

The investigation focused on one suspect, Charles H. Smithart, sixty-one, a retired laborer and handyman living in Copper Center. Smithart was born in Portland, Oregon, and had moved to Alaska in the early 1970s from Redding, California, to be near his mother and get in on the economic boom coming with construction of the trans-Alaska pipeline. With him were his wife and six children. Smithart got a good job on the pipeline and settled down to stay, but his wife moved back to Redding after a few years, taking the children with her. Smithart was the son of Lucille Brenwick, seventy-eight, a respected elder and president of the Copper River Native Association. Lucille lived in a trailer next to a garage apartment where Smithart lived.

Smithart was recognized early on as someone obsessively interested in the case and one of the first to volunteer for the search party. He told his friends about traveling the area's roads and sweeping the woods and fields with binoculars, looking for any sign of the girl. He even spent one afternoon talking nonstop as he drove a trooper through the network of roads near where the body later was found. After the discovery, even though police had released no information about the condition of the body or what might be missing, Smithart watched a circling helicopter taking aerial photos and commented to a trooper that he assumed it was looking for the girl's missing clothes.

Smithart had many friends, including his two ex-wives. Most were convinced that Smithart was motivated to search primarily by the twenty thousand dollars offered for information leading to the arrest and conviction of Mandy's killer. Because the entire community was focused on the case, Smithart was not the only one obsessed by the girl's disappearance, but detectives received other information that piqued their curiosity.

The first solid tip came from Dave DeForest, a truck driver and construction worker who knew Smithart. DeForest told troopers that he was driving south on the Richardson Highway when he saw Smithart's tan pickup truck driving slowly in the opposite lane. He saw Smithart behind the wheel and watched in his rear-view mirror as the pickup signaled and turned onto Tazlina Terrace Drive, where Mandy Lemaire lived. DeForest told the detectives that he saw Smithart make the turn about 3 P.M., minutes before Mandy disappeared.

Dave DeForest was a convicted felon who had come to Alaska from New York while still on probation for an attempted burglary. His tip might have been taken with a grain of salt, perhaps even put him on the suspect list, but his story was backed up. Charlie Smithart's cousin, Tanya Nutter, said in a state trooper interview that she saw her cousin's pickup two hours after the girl disappeared, just a mile from where Mandy's body was found. She couldn't confirm that Smithart was behind the wheel, but she was certain it was his truck.

Troopers went to Smithart's home with a warrant and questioned him intensely. They spent six hours searching for anything that might tie him to Mandy Lemaire's disappearance, especially looking for pink slacks, a red shirt, white tennis shoes, the back of an earring, photographs, hair and blood samples, newspaper clippings about the murder, rope or cord, diaries, and printed material related to abductions.

The officers seized Smithart's truck and searched it, too. They found two blond hairs and carefully removed several samples of red fiber. They went through

Smithart's shop, scraped and swept the floor, and took a blood-spattered paper towel that Smithart said he used when he cut his hand. They searched Lucille Brenwick's home for carpet fibers and went away with several rifles, including one .22 caliber weapon. Smithart's mother was furious. She told her friends that the guns had not been fired in years. She demanded that troopers account for every single .22 cartridge they took with them.

Charlie Smithart was flabbergasted and outraged. He said when the girl disappeared he was at home watching his favorite daytime television shows, "Wheel of Fortune" and "Jeopardy." He claimed to have two witnesses with him at the time. Smithart's flamboyant denials only increased police interest in him. His friend, Ed Church, told a neighbor, "I think Smithart has talked himself into the can."

Police suspicions surrounding Charlie Smithart became well known to area residents, in part because Charlie and his mother talked freely about it. He told more than one friend that when troopers asked for a sample of his pubic hair, he dropped his pants and said, "Help yourself."

Still, few if any of Charlie's family or friends thought he was capable of such a crime, assuming suspicion eventually would shift to someone else. Some were not so sure. On Halloween night, pranksters propped a plywood sign in Smithart's driveway that said: "Beware Psycho."

On November 26, troopers arrested Charlie Smithart in his apartment on charges of kidnapping, sexual assault, and first-degree murder. He was booked into the Mat-Su Pre-Trial Facility in Palmer and held on $450,000 bail. The arresting officers came for Smithart while his mother was away. When Lucille returned, she assumed Smithart was tinkering in the garage, and began cooking dinner. She didn't know he had been arrested until a reporter called. He was indicted by a grand jury and arraigned the next day in Palmer Superior Court. He pled not guilty to all charges.

In a jailhouse interview with the *Anchorage Daily News*, Smithart said he was a victim, that the real murderer was still free. He said Mandy never had been in his truck and that the blond hair found there likely was that of a friend's son. He said that if he had killed the girl, he would have dumped the body in the fast-flowing Copper River, not in the woods near her home. Smithart added that he didn't have bail money and, even if he did, wouldn't bail himself out for fear of "kooks and vigilantes" who wanted to kill him. He said he was better off in jail because the murderer likely would kill again, proving that he didn't kill Mandy Lemaire.

The evidence against Charlie Smithart was mostly circumstantial and hearsay, but much of it was convincing. Nothing tied him directly to the crime, not even DNA testing, which was inconclusive. A forensic scientist from Illinois testified that red fibers found on Mandy's body and on a pair of coveralls stuffed behind the seat of Smithart's pickup were identical, though the source of the fibers could not be established. A fellow prisoner testified that Smithart had confessed to him while both were awaiting trials. One of Smithart's five adult daughters told detectives that Smithart had molested her and her sisters when they were children.

Charlie Smithart went to trial in June 1993 in Anchorage. Some evidence was excluded for various reasons. His lawyer claimed that witness Dave DeForest, a convicted felon, was a proven liar whose testimony could not be trusted. He tried to argue that DeForest should be considered a suspect in the murder but the judge refused to allow it, saying no evidence existed tying DeForest to the crime. The defense lawyer acknowledged that his client was an eccentric with a rude and endlessly moving mouth, which attracted the interest of detectives, but insisted that his eccentricity did not make him a criminal.

When Tonya Nutter testified that she saw her cousin's pickup truck near Tazlina Terrace Drive the day Mandy disappeared, Smithart said sarcastically as she left the witness stand, "Thanks, Cuz."

Several young girls testified to strange encounters with Smithart in the weeks and months before Mandy disappeared — encounters in which he followed them in his truck while they rode their bicycles.

Smithart's incessant talking about young girls in a crude way did not help his case. During the trial, prosecutors submitted transcripts of his many conversations with troopers. In one, he talked about seeing an account of Mandy's disappearance and murder on "Unsolved Mysteries." Of the young actress who played Mandy, he said: "It ain't no eleven-year-old girl. If she is, she's sure got big tits on her for an eleven-year-old. Some gals eleven years old do have big tits; I've seen some that are starting them when they were nine years old that are getting developed like you can't believe. Hell, my ex-wife's sister, goddamn, well that whole family had tits on them like you couldn't believe when they were real young."

Several friends and relatives testified that they saw Smithart at his mother's place at the time the abduction took place six miles away, but their statements contradicted one another. Cash register receipts from a store showed that one of the alibi witnesses was lying. She was at the store when she said she saw Smithart at the trailer.

The jury found Charlie Smithart guilty of all charges. Smithart bellowed his outrage and was taken from the courtroom by guards and placed in an enclosed media booth while the jury was polled on its decision. He was sentenced to one hundred fourteen years in prison.

In 1999, the Alaska Supreme Court ordered a new trial for Smithart on the grounds that the trial judge had denied the defense lawyer the right to argue that Dave DeForest was the murderer. The court said the judge had set too high a bar for the defense by requiring that the lawyers submit convincing evidence that DeForest committed the crime. Before he could be retried, Charlie Smithart contracted lung cancer and died in prison.

In June 1992, while Smithart awaited trial, a male German shepherd named Mandy graduated from police training schools in Alabama and Alaska, then entered active service as a rookie in the Alaska State Troopers. The dog's police career was relatively short; he developed a leg problem after two years, retired, and was adopted by his handler as a family pet.

chapter thirteen

Death of a Maverick

---

*Joe Vogler thought Alaska should secede
from the union. When he disappeared, some
of his supporters thought the CIA or the
National Park Service had done him in.*

Joe Vogler was an eighty-year-old gold miner who
hated bureaucrats and environmentalists, whom he fa-
mously called "posy sniffers." His anger with the federal
government pre-dated Alaska statehood, originating
from an earlier time when many residents of the Territory of Alaska were disgusted by decisions made in far-
off Washington, D.C. by bureaucrats who had no un-
derstanding of life on the Last Frontier.

Vogler's fury was very personal. Much of it stemmed
from clashes with the feds over whether he had the right
to mine gold and drive his bulldozer over federal lands.
Because the federal government then owned virtually
all lands in Alaska, their prohibitions could be an im-

passable barrier to making a living by mining the precious metal that Alaska is known for.

Vogler came to Alaska from Kansas in 1942 after graduating from the University of Kansas law school, which he attended to please his father. He was unable to find work in Kansas and moved to Kodiak for a job on a military construction project. That was followed by a job helping build an airport runway at Northway. When the runway project ended, Vogler moved north, staked out a three-hundred-twenty-acre homestead near Fairbanks, and took up gold mining.

Joe Vogler thought Alaska should secede from the United States. He was serious about this idea and founded the Alaskan Independence Party. He was a high-profile character in the state's political scene, a three-time candidate for governor, whose trademarks were his fedora hat and booming voice. He and other members of his party participated in campaign political debates and one year the maverick party captured ten thousand votes, about five percent of the total. Few thought Vogler truly expected to be elected governor. But he did want his point of view to be heard and found that being a candidate gave him a seat at many forums.

His followers ranged from those who believed Washington was abridging states' rights, and therefore deserved to be told where to go, to those who passionately wanted Alaska to secede and form its own democratic government — one where an individual could be free. He once told an interviewer from the CBS program '60 Minutes': "I pledge my efforts, my effects, my honor, my life to Alaska. And to hell with America."

Throughout their adult lives, both Vogler and his, wife, Doris railed against Washington, saying it treated Alaska as a colony. Both vowed they would never be buried on American soil. When Doris died in 1992, Joe had her interred at Dawson in the Yukon Territory.

Trooper Captain John Myers in Fairbanks said of Vogler: "The guy is a folk hero up here. He's sort of Alaska's answer to Paul Bunyan or Pecos Bill, or whatever. Everyone in town knows him or knows of him, and everyone has a Joe Vogler story."

Vogler's temper was legendary, though as a secessionist he waged a war of words rather than violence. Author John McPhee wrote in his book *Coming Into the Country* that Vogler once said to the mayor of Fairbanks, "Get ready to look at this town for the last time, because I'm going to close your left eye with one fist and your right eye with the other."

On Friday, May 29, 1993, Joe Vogler had dinner with a friend who found him in good spirits and reasonable health for a man his age. People noticed Vogler had slowed somewhat since his wife's death. He missed her terribly. But he was still a visible presence in the community and active in politics. He had slicked-back gray hair and looked, as one writer put it, "like an elder Indiana Jones." Vogler was sometimes depressed and forgetful, too. He talked occasionally about ending his own life if he should become terminally ill but at other times it seemed as if he had not lost his unceasing optimism. His friend and AIP running mate, Al Rowe, said Vogler was dating a widow and seemed "about to pop the question." Rowe said Vogler was thinking of building a new house on the homestead he had occupied for fifty years. Vogler dropped by Rowe's place on Sunday, the afternoon before Memorial Day, to talk about clearing some land. "He was all excited about that." Rowe said, "God, he likes to drive a Cat. He wanted to get out there the next day."

Rowe dropped by to see Vogler two days later. Things didn't look right at all. Joe's Mercedes, pickup truck, and station wagon were parked outside the house, and his bulldozer was nearby. When Rowe honked his horn, he heard Vogler's five dogs barking inside. He went in through a side door and found the frantic dogs apparently hadn't been fed, watered, or let outside for several days. Vogler's pet goose was in its cage, covered by a blanket that Vogler customarily put in place before going to bed. The old man's wallet and heart medicine were on the kitchen table and his .44 handgun was on the bed. The only things missing were Vogler himself, a small .32 pistol he carried, and his gray fedora.

Rowe reported Vogler missing, touching off an investigation and an intensive search of the surrounding fields, wooded areas, and the wilderness beyond. He had vanished. No sign could be found — not by search dogs, searchers on horseback, a National Guard helicopter, or even dowsers who walked the ground with pendulums and wires watching for a telltale swing or bounce that would point the way to Vogler's body.

U.S. Senator Frank Murkowski asked the FBI to step in, but the agency declined on the grounds that it had no jurisdiction in a local case. Conspiracy theories abounded because Vogler had been an outspoken critic for so many years of all federal agencies, from the CIA to the National Park Service. Vogler's friends wondered if one of his enemies in high places had silenced him. Some thought he had been abducted or murdered because of his beliefs, though the grouchy politician actually was a revered figure in Alaska, even among people who disagreed with his radical views.

When no clues were turned up in the initial investigation, Vogler's friends pooled their resources and hired a private detective, putting out collection jars in banks and offices to raise money for a reward.

As the weeks went by with no break in the case, suspicions grew. Some of Vogler's followers were convinced it was a Washington-based plot. One FBI special agent, asked if the FBI or National Park Service might have taken Vogler, replied indignantly, "If we don't go kidnap someone like Saddam Hussein, we're certainly not going to go after Joe Vogler."

In late August, troopers revealed that they had several leads. Lieutenant Governor Jack Coghill said troopers had three suspects and were narrowing their focus. Coghill said two of the suspects were Alaskans and one was an Oklahoma man. In October, an Alaskan Independence Party official asked Fairbanks-area residents to search their properties one more time before winter set in. Within weeks a heavy blanket of white covered Interior Alaska and the search for Vogler's final resting place was reluctantly abandoned.

In February, the Alaskan Independence Party held its annual convention in a Wasilla hotel. One hundred party faithful attended the session in a classic smoke-filled room, but this time they found a table at the back of the room stacked with bumper stickers, T-shirts, and buttons, all asking, "Where's Joe?" A television played videos of his best-known speeches. Pictures of Vogler in his fedora were plastered on doors and walls. It was the party's first convention without its founder. Speeches were peppered with lines like, "I'm sure Joe would have ..." and "Joe would have wanted ..."

When the last of winter's snow melted in May, a year after Vogler's disappearance, state troopers, search dogs, and the Wilderness Search and Rescue group took to the field again. This time their efforts were concentrated in an old mining area called Skoogy Gulch off the Steese Highway north of Fairbanks. It was apparent they were working from specific information. Trooper Sergeant Jim McCann told reporters he planned to search until he found Vogler's body. The trooper was certain that finding the corpse would lead to the arrest of the killer. Though he offered no specifics, McCann said he was working on new angles and checking out hunches.

Jim McCann was a trooper legend, a relentless detective known for tracking down murderers and extracting confessions. One of his greatest talents was in questioning suspects and mentally putting himself in their shoes. He could see things from their point of view, sympathize with their plight, and become a friend who would help them in their desperate situation. He could keep them talking and get them to confide in him, to tell what they did and everything they knew.

The spring search turned up nothing new, but McCann had a good idea who had killed Vogler and had known almost from the start. Proving his case was another matter, but McCann was a dogged and talented investigator. He bided his time.

The suspect was in jail and presumably going nowhere. He had been arrested the previous October in Oklahoma on an Alaska check forgery charges and extradited back to the state. He had run to Oklahoma from Fairbanks after stealing fifty-five hundred dollars from his girlfriend's mother, signing the woman's name on the checks.

The suspect, Manfried West, was a thirty-eight-year-old sometimes sign-painter who once worked on a Vogler political campaign. While awaiting trial on the forgery charge, he was staying at a Fairbanks halfway house and serving the balance of a four-year term for an old burglary conviction. But on May 27, McCann learned that West had walked away from the halfway house and was missing. The trooper had a hunch that West might be staying at a cabin owned by West's stepbrother, who was working on a mining claim. McCann got a warrant to arrest West for escaping from the halfway house. He and a tactical team of six troopers drove to the stepbrother's cabin. As they approached, West stepped out the back door, saw them, and ducked back inside. He shouted that the officers had better not come near him because he was carrying a rifle and had explosives taped to his chest.

McCann used his cell phone to call the cabin, and West answered. It was a brief conversation by McCann's interview standards, less than four hours. Astonished reporters and editors listening in on a radio scanner at the Fairbanks Daily News-Miner overheard their conversation.

As the tactical team waited with guns ready, a helicopter hovered nearby, and newspaper reporters took notes, Jim McCann worked his magic on Manfried West. The detective listened sympathetically as West told him about his confrontation with Vogler. It was a robbery that did not go well. West threatened the old man with a .22 pistol but Vogler refused to turn over either gold or cash and ordered West off the property.

Vogler pulled his own pistol and fired a shot in the air. "I told you to get the fuck out of here," Vogler hollered, "and the next one I'm blowing your head off."

Vogler then took a shot at West's truck. The robber responded by firing at Vogler. The first shot missed and the second hit Vogler, though the light bullet didn't bring him down. Vogler turned and ran but West fired again and the old man fell dying.

West told McCann that he expected the sound of the shootout to bring police or neighbors. He waited fearfully and, when nobody came, loaded the body into his truck and drove to Nenana. He wrapped the old miner in a blue tarp, sealed it with duct tape, and buried it in a three-foot hole.

Though West grew increasingly erratic as the discussion went on, McCann tried to calm him and get him to surrender. In mid-evening, the waiting troopers saw smoke and flames coming from the cabin. Twice,

West ran outside with officers calling for him to give up. Both times he turned and ran back inside into the flames. Several small explosions were heard. Firemen arrived but were kept away from the cabin because of the threat of a larger explosion.

When the roof caved in, firefighters moved in, finding West safe in a small tunnel under a cinderblock wall, covered with soot. "It was unbelievable," McCann said later. "He looked dead, but then he started shaking."

McCann tried to get the conversation going again in a Fairbanks hospital, hoping to get the location of Vogler's grave, but West would go no further. "We talked and talked," McCann said, "and finally he said, 'Nah, I've got to talk to my lawyer.'"

In mid-October, troopers went to a Nenana gravel pit reportedly suggested to them by West's former cellmate. The grave was pinpointed by a cadaver-sniffing dog named Maya, and a little shoveling uncovered the remains of Alaska's most fractious politician.

Though Vogler never had held an elective office, Governor Walter J. Hickel ordered state flags lowered for three days of official mourning. Friends and admirers filled a church for his funeral service. The casket was covered with a large state flag and the proceedings ended with the crowd standing and singing "Alaska's Flag," the official state song.

A grand jury hearing in December 1994 revealed the reason for Jim McCann's suspicions about Manfried West. Darlene Dokken, manager of a Fairbanks trucking company, testified that she had heard West comment two months before Vogler's disappearance about a gold stash he had seen in the basement of Vogler's home. West told her, "You should have seen the stuff he had down there."

"As he was talking to me," Dokken told the grand jury, "it went through my mind: 'God, if anything ever happens to Joe Vogler, I'll call and turn in this guy.' "

Other grand jury testimony indicated West returned from Oklahoma four days before the Vogler killing. He flew to Anchorage where he borrowed a car and gas money. He told a friend that "he had to go and do somebody," and was going to erase a debt. West showed up at the woman's house several days after Vogler's disappearance.

"He was nervous," she said. "His face was real flush. He'd been sweating quite a bit."

West had left several guns, some cash, and a video camera with her. When troopers approached, she turned the items over. Tracing serial numbers, detectives learned that the camera had belonged to Vogler's late wife, Doris.

Manfried West was charged with first degree murder, robbery, and theft, but his lawyer plea-bargained on his behalf and West eventually was convicted of second-degree murder and evidence-tampering. He was sentenced to seventy-five years in prison.

Joe Vogler was buried beside his wife in a Yukon Territory cemetery, as he had directed, refusing even in death to make peace with America.

AUTHOR'S SOURCE NOTES

CHAPTER ONE
Ketchikan Burning

Federal Bureau of Investigation Report, "William Henry Mitchell, AKA Julia Dunton, Helen Monson, Unlawful Flight to Avoid Prosecution — Arson" dated November 13, 1963
"A Man Who Changed the Face of a City, The Firebug Bill Mitchell," by June Allen, *Sitnews*, Ketchikan, Alaska, November 15, 2002
Lew M. Williams Jr., retired publisher, *Ketchikan Daily News*, Lew Williams contributed information for this chapter and reviewed a draft
Ketchikan historian Louise Harrington
Wally Kubley, then a Ketchikan volunteer fireman and later a state legislator and commissioner of the Alaska Department of Commerce

CHAPTER TWO
Mystery of Mendeltna Lodge

Interview with Trooper Col. Tom Anderson
Interview with Trooper Detective Sergeant Don Church, CIB
Archives of *The Anchorage Times* and the *Anchorage Daily News*
Archives of Alaska Superior Court, Third Judicial District
Draft reviewed by Trooper Col. Tom Anderson

CHAPTER THREE
The Deadly Dentist

Interview with Trooper Investigator Corporal Dean Bivins
Archives of *The Anchorage Times* and the *Anchorage Daily News*
State of Alaska, Department of Law, press release dated January 26, 1968
The Alaska State Troopers Golden Anniversary – 50 Years of History, by Gerald O. Williams, chairman, Historical Committee, 1991

CHAPTER FOUR
The Cab Driver Killer

Interview with Alaska State Troopers Investigator Dean Bivins and Colonel Tom Anderson at Alaska State Trooper Museum
Archives of *The Anchorage Times* and *Anchorage Daily News*
Archives of Alaska Court System – Clerk of Courts
Notes of witness Nema Marine

CHAPTER FIVE
Murders at Jackass Creek

Interview with Trooper Col. Tom Anderson
Interview with Trooper Detective Dean Bivins
Interview with Trooper Major Walt Gilmour
Archives of *Anchorage Times* and the *Anchorage Daily News*
Archives of Alaska Judicial System
Archives of Alaska Department of Law, district attorney, Third Judicial District
Archives of Superior Court, Fourth Judicial District, Fairbanks, Alaska, warrant September 18, 1971 and Grand Jury indictment issued September 24, 1971
Draft reviewed by Trooper Col. Tom Anderson

CHAPTER SIX
The Search for Yellow 39

Interview with Trooper Col. Tom Anderson
Interview with Trooper Detective Sergeant Don Church, CIB
Archives of *The Anchorage Times* and the *Anchorage Daily News*
Alaska Supreme Court, opinion dated January 22, 1982 on appeal by Andrew Dolchok and various related documents

CHAPTER SEVEN
A Fairbanks Divorce

The Alaska State Troopers Golden Anniversary – 50 Years of History, by Gerald O. Williams, chairman, Historical Committee, 1991

CHAPTER EIGHT
Alaska's Billy the Kid

Archives of *The Anchorage Times* and the *Anchorage Daily News*
Johnny's Girl: A Daughter's Memoir of Growing Up in Alaska's Underworld, by Kim Rich, William Morrow and Co., 1993
Brief interview with Kim Rich
Interview with Trooper Sergeant Walt Gilmour, Criminal Investigation Bureau
Interview with Trooper Detective Sergeant Don Church, CIB
Interview with Trooper Sergeant Jim Vaden, CIB Major Crime Unit
Interview with Anchorage Detective Ron Rice, Anchorage Police Department
Alaska Court System, Third Judicial District, State of Alaska v. Gary Zieger, Case No. 72-500 Cr.

CHAPTER NINE
A Cold-Hearted Undertaker

Interview with Chief Investigator Sergeant Don Church
Archives of *The Anchorage Times* and the *Anchorage Daily News*
Archives of Alaska Court System, Third Judicial District
Alaska Department of Public Safety, Office of the Commissioner, Alaska State Troopers report dated March 14, 1974, D. D. Church, chief investigator, received after request under Public Records Act.
Draft copy reviewed by Trooper Church

CHAPTER TEN
An Angry Man

Interview with Special Agent Joseph A. Hanlon, Federal Bureau of Investigation, retired
Archives of *The Anchorage Times* and the *Anchorage Daily News*, 1976-87, especially 1985-87 articles by Sheila Toomey, Kim Rich, and Larry Campbell, *Anchorage Daily News*, and Rosanne Pagano, *Anchorage Times*
Archives of Alaska Court System – Clerk of Courts, arrest warrant dated November 11, 1985, for Neil S. MacKay, Larry Ray Gentry, John Ian Arthur Bright, Robert Allen Betts for murder in the first degree.
U.S. District Court, Magistrate's Docket No. A85-104 M, United States of America v Neil S. MacKay, affidavit of Joseph A. Hanlon, Special Agent, FBI, dated November 15, 1985 and referencing investigative report by Investigator Sergeant Michael Grimes, Anchorage Police Department

CHAPTER ELEVEN
Nightmare in a Ski Town

Interview with Alaska State Trooper Bill Hughes
Interview with Chris von Imhof, Alyeska Resort
Archives of the Department of Public Safety, Alaska State Troopers
Archives of Alaska District Court, Third Judicial District
Archives of *The Anchorage Times* and the *Anchorage Daily News*, courtesy of the *Anchorage Daily News*
Office of the District Attorney, Anchorage
Archives of Alaska Court System – Anchorage Clerk of Courts
Draft copy reviewed by Trooper Hughes and Chris von Imhof

CHAPTER TWELVE
A Young Girl is Missing

Archives of the *Anchorage Daily News*, including articles by the Associated Press

CHAPTER THIRTEEN
Death of a Maverick

Archives of *Anchorage Daily News*, including articles by the Associated Press and the *Fairbanks Daily News-Miner*

ABOUT THE AUTHOR

TOM BRENNAN is a newspaper editor and columnist based in Anchorage. Born in Massachusetts, he and his wife Marnie quit their jobs at a New England newspaper in 1967 and drove cross-country while towing a houseboat on wheels. It was a six-week journey that convinced them they didn't want to drive it both ways. In Anchorage, Tom became a reporter for *The Anchorage Times*, then worked for many years in the oil industry both as an in-house executive and external consultant. He became a writer for the *The Voice of The Anchorage Times* in 2000.

ABOUT THE ILLUSTRATOR

BRIAN SOSTROM studied art at Washington State University where he received a BFA. After graduation, he continued pursuing both illustrative and fine art. He has spent much of his professional career creating and designing artwork for video games. In 1997, he co-founded a Seattle-area development company where he is currently collaborating with other artists. Brian spends much of his spare time painting and pursuing outdoor interests.